AFFLICTED BUT NOT DESTROYED:

How God Used My Pain For My Purpose

DR. DARNELLA BENNETT

AFFLICTED BUT NOT DESTROYED:

Dedication

"I dedicate this memoir to everyone who has overcome barriers and countless obstacles to succeed. As the Bible says, 'I can do all things through Christ who strengthens me' (Philippians 4:13). For everyone who can genuinely say, 'If it had not been for the LORD who was on my side' (Psalm 124:1), this memoir is for you. For everyone who needs to know that God strategically designs everything we go through, and if we continue to walk the path that He has already chosen for us to follow, everything will work out for good; this memoir is for you. As Romans 8:28 says, 'And we know that in all things God works for the good of those who love him, who have been called according to his purpose.' Nothing is by coincidence. Everything is designed to happen the way it happens. Everything is orchestrated and ordained by God, Himself. This memoir is words and moments to bring encouragement to you. This memoir is dedicated to you."

Afflicted But Not Destroyed

How God Used My Pain For My Purpose

WE are Afflicted
In Every Way,
But NOT **Crushed;**

Perplexed,
But NOT **Despairing;**

Persecuted,
Bit NOT **Forsaken;**

Struck Down,
But NOT **Destroyed:**

II Corinthians 4: 8-9

Contents

Acknowledgments

COMPLETING THIS MEMOIR was only possible with the participation, involvement, and assistance of many people whose names may not be enumerated. Their contributions are sincerely appreciated. To all my relatives, church members, friends, and others who, in one way or another, shared their advice, moral support, and prayers, thank you. As the Bible says, 'I thank my God every time I remember you' (Philippians 1:3).

To my daughter, Dana, and my two grandchildren, Justin and Ashton, you will always be acknowledged in everything I do. You are my inspiration. I love you to the moon and beyond.

Above all, to God Almighty, the author and finisher of my faith, I thank Him for His love, guidance, and providence. Truly God's love is everlasting. As the Bible says, 'Give thanks to the LORD for he is good; his love endures forever' (Psalm 107:1).

I thank you.

Has God Chosen You?

When God wants to drill a man
And thrill a man
And skill a man,
When God wants to mold a man
To play the noblest part;
When He yearns with all His heart
To create so great and bold a man
That all the world shall be amazed,
Watch His methods. Watch His ways!
How He ruthlessly perfects
Whom He royally elects!
How He hammers him and hurts him,
And with mighty blows converts him
Into trial shapes of clay which
Only God understands;
While his tortured heart is crying
And he lifts beseeching hands!
How He bends but never breaks
When his good He undertakes;
How He uses whom He chooses
And with every purpose fuses him;
By every act induces him
To try His splendor out—
God knows what He's about!
— Anonymous

Deceptive Friends: How Darkness Tries to Abort God's Plan

"*K*AREN, LOOK WHAT Yvette gave me."

As I spoke with enthusiasm, I couldn't help but remember my recent conversation with Yvette, an upperclassman.

Yvette, a sophomore student, was often **called** "Duck" by her peers due to her unique walking step. She walked with her feet turned outwards, commonly known as "slue feet," which caused her to waddle like a duck when she walked.

I resided in the same dorm as Yvette at Rust College. Unbeknownst to me, she had been scheming against me. It wasn't going to be a harmless game but something more serious.

Rust College, located in Holly Springs, Mississippi, is a historically Black Institution of Higher Learning founded in 1866. It is the second oldest private college associated with the United Methodist Church. This educational institution is one of the HBCUs established by the Freedmen's Aid Society to educate black people after the Civil War. It was founded then and is still operational today, making it one of the ten institutions established during that period.

The week marked the end of classes before the final exams and summer break. It was a joyous moment for temporary goodbyes and well-wishes until school resumes in the fall. I enthusiastically walked through the dormitory hall, climbed the stairs to the sophomore residential area, then quickly turned to Yvette's room. She opened the door, smiled, and immediately said, "I have a special gift saved just for you!" Before I could say hello, Yvette eagerly exclaimed this message.

Yvette quickly veered from me and focused on the amber-colored medicine vial on her bookshelf. She held the container firmly with both hands and removed the white cap, exposing a white marijuana cigarette paper rolled up at both ends, commonly known as a joint.

Yvette's unexpected gift left me puzzled and curious. Why did she single me out from everyone else? What was the meaning behind her gesture? She insisted it was only for *me*, and I felt gratitude and suspicion. I thanked her politely but couldn't help wondering about the purpose of this special gift.

Someone had made something just for me, and this rare act of kindness moved me. This gesture touched my heart in a selfish world where people often grab more than they share. Yvette saw the happiness in my eyes and smirked wickedly at me! She knew that I had once smoked weed in a car with my ex-boyfriend, Ken, one evening when he drove back to the campus from Memphis. Ken was my first crush and a handsome guy in every way, but he enjoyed smoking weed from time to time.

When Ken and I arrived at the campus and walked through the dorm entrance, he dragged and slung my luggage down the dorm corridor with barely any awareness. I felt embarrassed and furious. That was the end of our night, and he hit the road again, bound for Memphis.

It was only a short time before he got stopped by the Mississippi Highway Patrol.

He feared a horrific night in jail for driving fast and having weed. This traffic stop was in the 70s, and Mississippi still had racist laws against blacks.

After they processed him, he got one phone call and picked me up. He said he was pulled over by the cops for speeding and was at the police station. Still high from the joint and mad that he tossed my luggage, I laughed and teased him: "They can put you under the ground as far as I'm concerned," I hung up the phone.

I felt proud that I had acted like a boss lady. I strutted back to my dorm room and slept as peacefully as a baby rocked in its cradle. "Rock A Bye, Baby!" I later told Yvette about the talk and the drama.

I didn't know that Yvette used this information to create a gift with its effects aimed at me. The words "just for me" kept echoing in my head as I took the vial.

She remarked that she knew it was the end of the semester and wanted to give me a parting gift before heading home for summer break. Again, I thanked her for her gesture and exited her dorm room. I had taken the bait. As I walked the corridor, her mysterious words *"Just for you"* rang louder and louder in the gut of my spirit.

I walked back to the first-year students' hall to show Karen the generous gift I had gotten and tell her more about it. When she saw the vial, Karen was thrilled and giggled like a girl hungry for a slice of cake. Karen rummaged through several drawers until she found a box of matches. Since her roommate was cramming for her finals, we decided to go to my room to smoke the joint. We left her room with the fire matches in hand.

We burst into my dorm room, laughing out loud. The idea of doing something wild, like smoking a joint in a dorm room, was thrilling, and the adrenaline pumping in me. It was still baffling that a popular sophomore hand-picked a freshman to award the forbidden prized possession-Just for you!

I removed the joint from its hidden case so Karen could light it with one of the matches. She took the first puff and then handed it to me. I took one hit off the joint. The smell of weed quickly filled the room, and the smoke slowly slipped under the door. I warned Karen, not wanting to get caught, "Girl, if this weed smell gets into the hall, the other students will snitch on us to the dorm mother." The dorm mother set up front and kept a watchful eye on the college residents residing at the dorm. She was the hall keeper. And I certainly did not want to be expelled from college, especially not for smoking marijuana.

I gestured for Karen to open the window. As I glanced at it, I was instantly startled and captivated by a dark, shapeless blob hovering outside, staring into the room. The jet-black, cloud-like figure drifted into the room. It was so black and devoid of light that it was impossible to see through it.

The dark figure slowly bobbed and floated through the open window. It kept drifting toward me until it vanished from my sight. I was the only one to see it.

Holding my head between both hands, I told Karen I felt funny. I wasn't giggling anymore; I suddenly felt frightened. I began to feel faint. I said to Karen, "Ooh, Karen. I need to lie down."

I desperately stumbled to the edge of the bed, clutching the sheets with the bit of energy I had left so I wouldn't crash to the concrete floor. That's all I remember. *Just for you!*

I felt like I was in "Wrinkle in Time." This phrase comes from a book I read in high school called A Wrinkle in Time. It's about a high-school girl named Meg who went on a journey through time and space. A mystique creature visits Meg and takes her to a tesseract—a "wrinkle" in space and time. A tesseract is a way of traveling through time and space.

This wrinkle and tesseract caused by the mystical creature brought Meg to the fifth dimension. Unlike Meg, I don't know if I was in the fourth, fifth, or sixth dimension; but I know this jet-black blob seemed to take me to a world or dimension of total darkness, and time froze like a wrinkle that couldn't be explained. How long? I don't know.

When I regained consciousness, I felt disconnected from my surroundings. I was in the room, but I wasn't feeling myself--the sweet, thoughtful, and intellectual, Darnella. A bizarre experience!

But we know that the devil has been the mastermind of harm and deception since the dawn of creation. He deceived Adam and Eve in the Garden of Eden. Everything has stayed the same since then, only the tools and people he uses to carry out his wick plan. He comes cunningly and offers a bait that looks appealing and harmless, but once we take a bite or cross that dangerous line, it becomes a whole different story.

But why would the devil in the form of a witch –Yvette– want to hurt me by creating and conjuring up that dark blob and sending it to my room? No harm came to Karen, mind you. It was only me.

Just for me…! Just for ME…!! JUST……. FOR… ME…!!!

The words started to ring louder and louder. This event was not a coincidence. I was the devil's specific target.

"Now the serpent was more crafty than any other beast of the field that the LORD God had made. He asked the woman, "Did God actually say, 'You shall not eat of any tree in the garden'?" And the woman said to the serpent, "We may eat of the fruit of the trees in the garden, but God said, 'You shall not eat of the fruit of the tree that is in the midst of the garden, neither shall you touch it, lest you die.'" But the serpent said to the woman, "You will not surely die. God knows that when you eat of it, your eyes will be opened, and you will be like God, knowing good and evil." So when the woman saw that the tree was good for food and that it was a delight to the eyes, and that the tree was to be desired to make one wise, she took of its fruit and ate, and she also gave some to her husband who was with her, and he ate. Then their eyes were opened, and they knew that they were naked. And they sewed fig leaves together and made themselves loincloths."—Genesis 3:1-7

Little did Adam and Eve know that fig leaves could not cover their sin and disobedience toward God. Without the shedding of blood, there is no forgiveness of sin. The Bible says God made coats of skin and clothed them. This compassionate act of God foreshadowed Jesus, who would shed his innocent blood on the cross and become the sacrificial lamb of God for the remission of our sins. We cannot thank God enough for His grace and mercy and for sending His only begotten Son. For God so loved the world that He gave His only begotten Son, that whosoever believeth in him should not perish, but have everlasting life.--St. John 3:16

The devil tempted Adam and Eve because he wanted to ruin God's divine purpose and plan for them. Again, nothing has changed with the devil. The Bible also says we are not ignorant of the enemy's devices. Therefore, likewise, the devil wants to ruin God's purpose and plan for our lives. Some of us have been called and chosen from our mother's womb to do great work in God. And the devil knows this.

But again, why me? Why would the devil specifically try to derail, harm, and stop me?

The devil's device was wicked, but underneath the enemy's plan, a more excellent plan was set in motion by God.

Afflicted but not destroyed. This memoir is about how God used my painful experiences to bring forth my purpose--BUT GOD!

7

꧁꧂

CHAPTER 1

The Prophecy: How God Revealed His Purpose and Plan for My Life

"Before I formed you in the womb, I knew you; before you were born, I set you apart...."
Jeremiah 1:5

THE CLOCK WAS ticking toward six o'clock on a Friday evening, and Auntie was nervously getting ready for a dinner date with her boyfriend. She had been looking forward to this night for weeks, hoping to impress him with her new dress and perfume.

She daydreamed about his compliments and kisses when her mother barged into her room, shattering her fantasies by announcing, "You have to cancel your plans and babysit your nieces and nephews. Your big sister is in labor and must go to the hospital now." "Of all the days, why did she have to choose Christmas?" Auntie protested.

Auntie was my birth mother's younger sister, and she was furious that she had to sacrifice her romantic evening to care for her nephews and nieces. Surely not Christmas!

Christmas was the day I was born. That was the day I came into this world. I was the first baby born at John Gaston Hospital in Memphis, Tennessee, on December 25 of that year. My birth mother never forgot that detail because the doctor who delivered me told her that she would receive a washing machine from the hospital as a prize for having the first newborn that Christmas morning. Years later, when she told me this story, she joked that she was still waiting for that washing machine. And she is still waiting.

My birth mother's name was Dorothy Mae. She did not raise me. I respectfully call her my birth mother because I owe her honor. She carried me in her womb for nine months and gave me the gift of existence.

She was a former beauty queen with a melodious voice. She displayed this talent in the pageant and won. I admired her ability to make people laugh with her witty and hilarious jokes. She often told these jokes and made comical faces with each phrase. She was hilarious.

She was a woman who walked with a confident swagger. She swayed her hips in a way that made men turn their heads for a second glance. Some men even stared. She was a beautiful, funny, and talented woman. But she also had a dark side. One of my aunts told me that my birth mother suffered a lot in her childhood and early adulthood. She also confided in me about some painful events that scarred her soul. The extent of some of the unfortunate events affected her emotional stability and prevented her from forming close bonds with her family and children.

After I reunited with my birth mother as an adult, she shared some of her hardships as a young mother. She told me the family lived in a cramped room above a "nickel and dime" store on the corner of East Pontotoc Street and Vance, near downtown Memphis, Tennessee. We barely had enough money to survive and often went hungry for days.

The food we could afford or scrounge was not enough to fill the stomachs of growing children. One of my sisters told me she once dreamed of a juicy turkey leg to ease the hunger gnawing at her belly on Thanksgiving Day.

My birth mother was under tremendous stress, especially since she was expecting another child any day. She realized she had no income or resources for her children's basic needs. She desperately needed a miracle to feed, clothe, and shelter them. She had no one to turn to for help - But God!

My birth mother was religious and tried to put her faith in Christ during those difficult times. Her faith led her to a prayer meeting at the Pentecostal Temple of the Church of God in Christ (COGIC) under Presiding Bishop J. O. Patterson, Sr., in Memphis, Tennessee. The church was founded in 1907 as a Pentecostal Holiness Organization and is acclaimed to be the most prominent Pentecostal Movement in the United States, with branches in 112 countries worldwide.

The movement was born out of the Azuza Street Revival in Los Angeles, California, in the early 1900s. A group gathered and experienced a mighty outpouring of the Holy Spirit, similar to Acts 2:1-21.

Extraordinary and inexplicable miracles began to happen. Many were healed, and blind eyes became open. The congregation began to speak in 'unknown tongues' as the Holy Spirit gave them utterance and interpretation. The Azuza Street Revival is most widely known for this ecstatic utterance—speaking in tongues.

Out of this movement came the Pentecostal Movement, with its roots in Memphis, Tennessee, with the establishment of the Pentecostal Temple and the Pentecostal Holiness Organization.

Pentecostal Temple was a short walk from my family's humble home above the corner store. One day, my birth mother felt a divine nudge to attend a prayer meeting there. As she entered the sanctuary, an old missionary with a fiery anointing approached and prayed for her.

The missionary placed her hands on my mother's belly and spoke words of prophecy over her. She declared that the child my mother was carrying in her womb would be set apart for a particular purpose and would not be like her other children. The missionary also revealed through the Holy Spirit that my birth mother would have a girl and told her so. My birth mother was amazed and uplifted by the missionary's words and kept them in her heart.

Soon after, my birth mother gave birth to a healthy baby girl on December 25, the same year of the prophecy. She named me Darnella, after my father, Darnell. I was a fast learner and a quick mover. I skipped the crawling stage and started walking when I was only six months old. It was clear that I was different from the rest. I was ahead of the curve right from the start. I even skipped a grade during my first year in public school by skipping kindergarten and being allowed by the school to enroll in first grade. The prophecy was coming to pass and showing in my life.

My birth mother did her best to care for her children, but life was too hard for her; she always struggled to make ends meet. The food and money ran out quickly and did not cover all the needs. Someone contacted the Juvenile Court System. And we, her children, had a short stay in Juvenile Court.

My godmother told me that when my father found me and saw me in Juvenile Court, I had no shoes on. He lifted me from the cold concrete floor and held me close to his chest. He had enough.

He decided to step in and help her by taking me in to live with him and his wife while her other children reminded with her. I was my father's only child at the time. He had me in his later years, and I was a girl--Daddy's girl.

But as time went by, resentment grew within and among my siblings because of the circumstances that led to my separation. It was like the story of Joseph, whom his father loved. He was a child of his old age and was born by Rachel, whom Jacob deeply loved.

"This is the account of Jacob. When Joseph was seventeen years old, he was tending the flock with his brothers, the sons of his father's wives Bilhah and Zilpah, and he brought their father a bad report about them.

Now Israel loved Joseph more than his other sons because Joseph had been born to him in his old age, so he made him a robe of many colors. When Joseph's brothers saw that their father loved him more than any of them, they hated him and could not speak kindly to him.

Then Joseph had a dream, and when he told it to his brothers, they hated him even more. He told them, "Listen to this dream I had: We were binding sheaves of grain in the field, and suddenly my sheaf rose and stood upright while your sheaves gathered around and bowed down to mine."

"Do you intend to reign over us?" his brothers asked. "Will you rule us?" So they hated him even more because of his dream and his statements.

Then Joseph had another dream and told it to his brothers. "Look," he said, "I had another dream, and this time the sun, moon, and eleven stars were bowing down to Me." He told his father and brothers, but his father rebuked him, saying, "What is this dream you have had? Will your mother, brothers, and I bow down to the ground before you?" And his brothers were jealous of him, but his father kept what he said in mind.

At a later time, Joseph's siblings were tending to their father's livestock in Shechem. "Prepare yourself; I will send you to check on them," said his father.

"I am ready," Joseph replied.

Then Israel told him, "Go now and see how your brothers and the flocks are faring, and bring word back to me."

So he sent him off from the Valley of Hebron. And when Joseph arrived in Shechem, a man found him wandering in the field and asked, "What are you looking for?"

"I am looking for my brothers," Joseph replied. "Can you please tell me where they are pasturing their flocks?" "They have moved on from here," the man answered. "I heard them say, 'Let us go to Dothan.'" So, Joseph set out after his brothers and found them at Dothan.

Joseph's brothers saw him in the distance and plotted to kill him before he arrived. "Here comes that dreamer!" they said to one another. "Come now, let us kill him and throw him into one of the pits. We can say that a vicious animal has devoured him. Then we shall see what becomes of his dreams!"

When Reuben heard this, he tried to rescue Joseph from their hands. "Let us not take his life," he said. "Do not shed his blood. Throw him into this pit in the wilderness, but do not lay a hand on him." Reuben said this to rescue Joseph from their hands and return him to his father. So, when Joseph came to his brothers, they stripped him of his robe—the robe of many colors he was wearing—and took him and threw him into the pit. Now the hole was empty, with no water in it.

And as they sat down to eat, they saw a caravan of Ishmaelites coming from Gilead. Their camels carried spices, balm, and myrrh to Egypt.

Then Judah said to his brothers, "What profit will we gain if we kill our brother and cover up his blood? Let us sell him to the Ishmaelites and not lay a hand on him; for he is our brother, our flesh." And they agreed. So when the Midianite traders passed by, his brothers pulled Joseph out of the pit and sold him for twenty shekels of silver to the Ishmaelites, who took him to Egypt.

When Reuben returned to the pit and saw that Joseph was not there, he tore his clothes, returned to his brothers, and said, "The boy is gone! What am I going to do?" Genesis 37:2-30.

Sibling jealousy and rivalry are problematic at home. Also, the alleged tendency to have a favorite child is not uncommon, especially when the circumstances surrounding the birth of a particular child are out of the ordinary. Joseph's brothers hated him because he was Daddy's favorite child, having been born out of extraordinary circumstances to a man in his old age by the wife he truly loved—a once barren woman—Rachel.

Joseph himself did not help with matters either. I must admit that in my dilemma and setbacks with my family. As a young adult, I only sometimes used wise discretion. I talked and shared private information with the wrong people at the wrong time. Joseph was young and imprudent, so when he shared his God-given dreams with his brothers, they detested him even more and plotted to kill him. You cannot tell everyone your dreams and aspirations.

Thus, like Joseph, my brothers and sisters have always been envious of me because I was different. I was the one whom they could not understand, define, or confine because there was a prophecy at work even before I was born and yet in my mother's womb.

I experienced many heartaches and endured a lot at the hands of my siblings. For example, when our shared mother passed on, they conspired and ensured I would receive nothing (not even a hat) from her estate. Even though I often paid her a visit at the hospital and was the only child to relieve her discomfort in the hospital bed.

As a double amputee, she could not leave the hospital bed without assistance, nor could she leave the room. During this time, I watched her for signs of depression or Post Traumatic Stress Disorder (PTSD). I would ask her if she knew who I was, and I would wait until she replied and reassured me that she did. Then I would wait to see the sparkle in her eyes and hear her chuckle at me, inquiring about such a dumb query. I knew then she was alert and still Mrs. Dorothy Mae—my birth mother. We went on excursions in the hospital as I would ask the nurses and hospital attendants to transfer her from the energy-zapping bed to a wheelchair carefully. And off on an adventure we would go. I feel relieved knowing I was with her during her final time here.

In addition, I was on the obituary program and spoke final words of love about her during the homegoing ceremony. It was heartwarming to spell out every letter of her name DOROTHY and give a heart-warming message for each letter of her character. I loved and appreciated her for bringing me into the world.

I wished she could have been more admirable and selfless enough to embrace the daughter God had returned to her life. Unfortunately, she appeared more focused on the trials and tribulations she had incurred than the open door and gift God restored in her life—her child. Her verbal and physical attacks out of anger were in perpetuity. It is sad to be blind to the mercies and grace of God, to turn a deaf ear to his loving-kindness. And to close a hand in receiving God's gift.

Anger is a dangerous weapon of the enemy. The Bible says to "be angry but do not sin." When we allow our anger to make us bitter, unforgiving, hateful, and critical, we "give the devil a foothold" (Ephesians 4:26-27).

Unforgiveness stemming from anger can be a weapon of the enemy and a stronghold that can bite at our souls and destroy relationships. The LORD's prayer recites, "LORD, forgive me as I forgive others that transgress against me." We must learn to forgive others as we want the LORD to forgive us.

But one crucial person we leave out of the forgiveness equation is ourselves, whom we must also learn to forgive. We must show ourselves mercy and grace, and kindness. Sadly, this was the downfall of my birth mother, and this lack of self-love and forgiveness hindered a mother-daughter relationship. She could not forgive herself, and the unwarranted and unmerited guilt she carried spilled out as anger. It sabotaged the possibility of a nurturing and peaceful relationship with me, my father, and the woman who reared her child.

Sometimes out of unwarranted guilt, the enemy prompted her to speak derogatory remarks against the woman who sacrificed so much to raise her child. Out of anger, she reacted unkindly against my father's helping nature and hand, who did everything possible to help ease her burden during the struggling and financially unstable times.

Again, it is a must that we forgive. Unforgiveness is like cancer eating away at the soul. The only person the cancer damages is those infected with the bad cells, but these bad cells spread and increase. And so does the lousy spirit of unforgiveness. Therefore, we must learn to forgive others and, most importantly, ourselves. Let it go; your circumstances warranted it. You are a better version of yourself today.

It can also be like a venom that can be poisonous. This venom can be supplanted into and throughout the family, creating an ugly spirit of jealousy and hatred among family members, God forbid, the innocence of the children. Father, I pray that we all share in your Spirit of forgiveness for others and ourselves - in Jesus' name.

The catch-22 about my birth mother and our relationship was that I understood her pain and suffering and prayed for an opportunity to share a mother-and-daughter relationship with her. I wanted and needed to hear from her. To listen to her heart of guidance through a rough patch.

The LORD never makes a mistake, and His timing is perfect. I, too, was suffering when God brought us back together.

God knew when He reunited us; I needed someone in my life who knew how to suffer and would be able to witness to me. I needed someone to testify that God was a deliverer and a very present help in times of trouble. Many are the affliction of the righteous, but the LORD will deliver us out of them all (Psalm 34:19).

What more befitting person than a mother to reassure us of this hope and faith in the LORD? Especially a mother who experienced extreme suffering and knew that nobody but God brought her through the pain and heartaches.

I kept yearning and praying that she would tell me everything would be OK. Keep reading this memoir and see how these words finally came to fruition.

I knew of her struggles but yearned and needed to hear how the LORD had made way for her, how He was a very present help in times of trouble, and how he could provide water in dry places and calm the raging sea. I needed to see God and His workmanship. Let me see God in you—I yearned.

The Bible says that we overcome adversities by the Blood of the Lamb and the words of our testimony. I longed to hear her testimony. I see the person who once struggled, but I need your testimony. I do not need to listen to all the endless rehashing of pain and sorrows. I do not need to see you continuously wallowing in guilt and shame. If anyone is in Christ, he is a new creation; old things have passed away, and look, new things have come (II Corinthians 5:17). All I need to hear and know--is there a word from the LORD?

God sent me back to her at this appointed time. But hate never bonds two people; only love and kindness can do that. Yea, I have loved thee with an everlasting love; therefore, with loving kindness have I drawn thee (Jeremiah 31:3). It was the perfect time for her to be a mother and mend the wounds of a broken daughter's heart and be a witness to the almighty power of God.

God never makes a mistake, and he orchestrates our paths. People are moved out and into our lives for an appointed reason and a season. We must learn to trust God even when we cannot track Him. But know His timing and placement are perfect. We must learn to open our hearts to new possibilities, opportunities, and loving relationships. Our God yet sits on the throne and is in control.

Sibling jealousy and rivalry can cause much trouble in a family. It can also be worse when there is a perceived notion of a favorite child, especially when the child is born under unusual circumstances.

Joseph's brothers hated him because he was his father's favorite son, born to him in his old age by the wife he loved the most - Rachel, who was barren for a long time. Joseph did not help his situation either. I must admit that I made similar mistakes with my siblings. As a young adult, when we all reunited, I was not always wise or discreet. I talked and shared private information with the wrong people at the wrong time.

Joseph was young and naive, so when he told his brothers about his dreams of God, they despised him even more and planned to kill him. You cannot trust everyone with your dreams and goals.

So, like Joseph, my brothers and sisters have always been envious of me because I was different. I was the one they could not figure out, label, or limit because there was a prophecy at work in my life even before I was born.

For this, I suffered many hurts and hardships at the hands of my siblings. For instance, when our mother passed away, they conspired to ensure I would get nothing (not even a hat) from her estate even though I visited her often at the hospital and was the only child who comforted her in the confinement of the four walls of her hospital room. I would ask the nursing staff on duty for permission to take her on excursions around the hospital in her wheelchair so she could relieve herself from only being confined to her hospital room. Her face beamed with delight.

She had lost both legs and could not leave the bed or room without assistance. I watched her for signs of depression and post-traumatic stress, which could easily slip in with losing both limbs. I would ask her if she knew who I was and wait for her to answer. Then I would see the sparkle in her eyes and hear her laugh at my silly suggestion. Of course, I know who you are—Darnella. I'm glad I was with her during her last days here.

I spoke at her funeral and shared loving words about her. It was touching to spell out every letter of her name DOROTHY and give a heartfelt message for each letter of her personality.

I appreciated her for giving me life. I wished she could have been more loving and selfless enough to embrace the daughter God had brought back into her life. But she seemed more focused on the problems and pains she had gone through than the opportunity and gift God had given back to her - her child.

Anger filled her words with bitterness. It's sad to be blind to God's mercy and grace, to turn a deaf ear to his kindness, and to close a hand to his gifts and blessings. Anger is a dangerous weapon of the enemy. The Bible says, "Be angry but do not sin." When our anger makes us bitter, unforgiving, hateful, and critical, we "give the devil a foothold" (Ephesians 4:26-27).

Unforgiveness stemming from anger is a weapon of the enemy and will eventually become a stronghold that can eat away the joy in our souls to destroy relationships. The Lord's prayer says, "LORD, forgive us our debts as we forgive our debtors." We must learn to forgive others as we want the Lord to forgive us. But one vital person we often forget to forgive is ourselves. We must also learn to forgive ourselves. We must show ourselves mercy, grace, and kindness.

Sadly, this was my birth mother's downfall, and this lack of self-love and forgiveness also crippled our mother-daughter relationship. She could not forgive herself, and her guilt spilled over as anger. But somehow, we make it through. I prayed and yearned for a more peaceful relationship. But in due time, God will answer this request. It will be a miracle, and God will orchestrate it, as you will see—But God!

༄༅༅༅

CHAPTER 2

Born Date: All Part
of God's Plan

*Y*OU MIGHT WONDER why you were born on a specific date, just like I did. But there is no coincidence or randomness in this. It is all part of God's plan for our lives. He has a purpose and a destiny for each of us, revealing them to us through His spiritual laws and principles. We can align ourselves with His will and ways when we understand His spiritual mysteries.

One of these mysteries is the spiritual portal that opens when we enter this world. Not just our physical body that comes out of our mother's womb, but our spirit also comes from Heaven. Our spirit is the essence of who we are, the breath of life God gave us when He created us in His image. Our mother may have given birth to us, but God gave us our spirit. The Bible says, "God is spirit, and his worshipers must worship him in the Spirit and truth." (John 4:24). Our spiritual existence from birth stems from God.

Let's consider this point by observing the pros and cons of solely basing our existence on the family we were born into. Establishing the essence of our existence solely on our family can be a good thing, especially when we are born into a tight-knitted or influential family. However, it can be tricky when we exclusively base our existence in this world on the dynamics of the family unit.

Family dynamics shape our identity, values, relationships, and well-being. However, our existence is not exclusively based on family dynamics but on other factors such as our culture, religion, education, experiences, and choices. Family dynamics are not static but change over time and across generations. Therefore, basing our existence on family dynamics can be tricky because they are complex, diverse, and dynamic.

Even family resemblance can be a tricky thing. Sometimes, you can look at a person and see their parents, siblings, or relatives in their features, gestures, or expressions. Someone might say, "You have your mother's eyes," or "You smile just like your uncle." We make These everyday observations when we notice physical similarities among family members. But these similarities do not always reflect a person's personality or spirit. The body is just a vessel that our spirit inhabits for a while.

I know what it is like to have siblings who are very different from me and from each other. I am sure some of you can relate to that. Even twins can sometimes be different and completely the opposite of each other. Occasionally, we may feel like we don't belong to our biological family or have nothing in common with them. We may feel like strangers or outsiders in our own homes. This sense of isolation can be a lonely and painful feeling. But there is hope and comfort in knowing that we have another family - a spiritual family.

When we are born again through the Spirit of God, we become part of His family. We are connected to Him and to all those who share His Spirit. We may find more affinity and harmony with our spiritual kin than our blood kin. We may discover more similarities in spiritual values and beliefs than physical traits.

It would help if you didn't think I was dismissing or devaluing the importance of biological family connections. I know that they are a blessing and a gift from God. I also know that some of you may feel lonely or rejected by your families. You may need to fit in or be loved or accepted. I want you to know that you are not alone. You have a heavenly Father who loves and is always with you unconditionally. You have His Spirit within and beside you, guiding and comforting you. You don't have to worry about anything; He will care for you and your family. He will work everything out for your good. Just trust in Him and His promises.

Finally, let me share another spiritual mystery related to our birthdates. Did you know that our spiritual portal only opens once a year? That's why our birthdays are so special and meaningful. They celebrate our biological age and remind us of our spiritual origin. They mark the day Heaven opened up to release our spirit into this world. On our birthday, God gives us a special grace, a unique and personal blessing.

To further illustrate the birthday's importance and how it is an opportunity for a special blessing from God, I will share an experience and my daughter's testimony.

I will never forget when my daughter was looking for a house. It was one of the most challenging times of her life. She had just left a toxic relationship and moved to Nashville, hoping for a fresh start. But things went differently than planned. The company that hired her phased out the position on the day she arrived to report to work, leaving her without a job. She had no choice but to relocate to Murfreesboro, where she found a lovely duplex to rent.

The duplex had a large lake in the back, and she could sit on her terrace to watch the geese and deer as they gazed and drank water from the lake. But her landlord turned out to be a nightmare. He was having an affair and refused to renew the duplex's lease at the end of the term. My daughter had lived at the residence for three years and sometimes paid the rent three months in advance. His demented refusal was solely based on his hidden motive to move in with his mistress. He gave her only two weeks to find another place after her lease expired.

My daughter was homeless and desperate. She signed up for the Salvation Army program for women, but they could only offer her a bed for a few nights at a time. She had to bounce from one hotel to another, spending more money than she could afford. Most hotels were nicely accommodating, but some needed to be updated. She finally settled in an extended-stay hotel that was decent and affordable.

That's when she told me that the LORD had spoken to her spirit and comforted her. God told her that this was only a temporary trial and that He had a better plan for her. He told her she would look back on this experience and laugh one day. He told her He would restore everything she had lost and fill her heart with joy.

God prepared a special blessing for my daughter amid the storm. She was preapproved, and God opened a door for her to buy a house.

She invited me to join her in checking out a house she liked. It was in a pleasant rural close-knitted neighborhood. As we drove through the surrounding areas, I saw no African-Americans. We went closer to the home, and I noticed a large gas station that seemed to service most of the community; I glanced and scanned the lot, but still, I did not see any African-Americans on site. Not seeing people of color was a bit concerning for me; this was a rural community close to a city called Lynchburg. There were no people here that looked like my daughter. I silently prayed, "LORD, please don't let these folks lynch my family." The LORD put peace in my spirit.

We arrived at the house. As soon as we walked into the house, I was amazed by its spaciousness. It had everything that my daughter wanted and needed. She loved cooking and entertaining guests, and the house had a spacious, modern kitchen and a large dining area with beautiful bay windows that let in plenty of natural light. I was impressed by the house's design and layout.

But what caught my eye was the main bedroom and its bathroom. The bedroom had a cozy fireplace that added warmth and charm. The bathroom had a stand-alone waterfall shower that looked relaxing and refreshing. It gave the vibe of "Calgon, take me away!"

But the most stunning feature was the jacuzzi tub under a grand chandelier. It was like something out of a magazine or a movie. I knew this was the house God had prepared for my daughter. This was the house that He wanted to bless her with.

I immediately stepped out of the bathroom, leaving my daughter and the real estate agents in the room; their presence did not matter anymore. I needed to talk with Jesus; that was all that mattered now. With my hands lifted to God, I prayed, "God, do it for my daughter." "LORD, grant her this house." "God, you said double for our troubles."

I thought about all the hardships she had endured, the nights she had no place to call home, and all the times she had to sleep in hotels and a shelter. All the tears she had shed and how she maintained her strength and dignity amid the storm.

I remembered how I had once slept in one of the hotel bathtubs so that my grandchildren could have the bed to themselves. It was the smallest and most challenging concrete tub I had ever seen.

I suffered sleeping in the hard concrete tub that night but did it for my daughter and her children. We make sacrifices for our children and grandchildren. But God makes miracles for them.

The chandelier over the jacuzzi tub spoke volumes to me. No more hard small tubs! It showed God's favor and grace over my daughter's life.

God did it! He blessed my daughter with the house.

She called me one day and said, "You won't believe when the closing date is!" I asked her eagerly, "When is it?" She said, "August 17!" That was her birthday. Her spiritual portal day. The day when God released her spirit into this world. The day when God released an extraordinary blessing for her. He gave her a double portion of the gift, signed and officially released on her birthday. He gave her a new house, and her joy returned. God makes everything beautiful in his time (Ecclesiastes 3:11).

Our birthday is not just a random date on the calendar. It is a momentous day that marks the beginning of our journey on Earth. It is the day God opened a portal for our spirit to enter this world. That day opens opportunities for God to grant us a special grace and pour out a unique and personal blessing.

He gave us a purpose and a destiny that He wants us to fulfill. He gave us a mission and a calling that He wants us to pursue. He gave us a reason and a meaning for our existence.

Many people seek guidance and direction from sources other than God. They turn to horoscopes or astrology to find out what the stars have in store for them. They rely on human wisdom or worldly standards to measure their success and happiness. They chase after money and material things to fill the emptiness in their hearts. But they need to include the point of life. They are missing the essence of life. Life is not about how much we have or how well we do in the eyes of others. Life is about how well we do in the eyes of God. Life is about finding fulfillment in Him and His will for us.

Fulfillment comes from discovering and living out our God-given spiritual gifts. Satisfaction comes from serving and blessing others with what God has given us. Realization comes from following Jesus and His example of love, grace, and truth. Jesus said he came to give us life and life more abundantly (John 10:10).

He also said that whoever wants to save their life will lose it, but whoever loses their life for His sake will find it (Matthew 16:25). He taught us that the greatest among us is the one who serves the most (Matthew 23:11). He showed us that money is not evil. Still, it is not our master either (Matthew 6:24). He showed us that money is a tool that we can use to advance His kingdom and help His people (Luke 16:9). He showed us that money is not something that we can take with us when we die, but something that we can invest in eternal treasures (Matthew 6:19-21).

The devil knows our purpose and destiny better than we do. He knows our potential and our power in Christ. He knows that we are a threat to his plans and schemes. That's why he attacks us from the moment we are born. He tries to stop us, distract us, deceive us, discourage us, or destroy us. He makes us doubt our identity, value, worth, or calling. He tries to make us forget who we are and whose we are.

I experienced this firsthand when my daughter was born. She was a sweet baby, a gift from God. But she was also a target of the enemy. During labor, my body went into fetal distress. My daughter was not getting enough oxygen through the placenta. The heart monitor showed that her heartbeat was dropping rapidly. The doctor ordered an emergency cesarean section to deliver her safely and to save her life. The enemy tried hard to stop her destiny in the womb, even before birth. Being born threatens the devil when you have a calling, and God's hand is on your life.

She came out of my womb healthy and beautiful, weighing 6 pounds and 7 ounces. But she had a minor defect in her stomach that might require surgery later on. But she was alive and well, thanks to God's grace and protection.

However, the devil was not done with trying to harm her. He knew that she was precious, and he wanted to destroy her. He attacked her digestive system, making her unable to eat or digest food properly. She would vomit everything she swallowed, sometimes with such force that it would splatter on the wall. It was a horrible sight for a small child to go through this kind of spiritual warfare. The devil does not play fair. He hits us where it hurts the most. He does not care about our age or our condition.

One day, the situation got worse. My daughter's intestines got twisted and blocked. Food could not get into her stomach or out of her bowels. She was in pain and distress. We rushed to the LeBonheur Children's Hospital in Memphis. The doctors in the emergency room examined her and decided that she needed surgery right away. They called the head surgeon at his home and told him to come to the hospital as soon as possible.

The head surgeon arrived around 3:00 a.m. He was an older white man, and I could sense that he was a man who knew God. He glowed on his face and had a calmness in his spirit. He told me he disliked operating on young children, especially when they are so small. My daughter was two years old then but could not grow and thrive due to food not digesting correctly and remaining in her stomach.

He suggested we wait two or three days to see if medication and observation would resolve the problem. He said that he would only do surgery as a last resort. I agreed to his plan, and we stayed in the hospital for three days. I remained in the hospital with my daughter to closely monitor her condition and comfort her.

The hospital staff was kind and attentive but could not do much to help my daughter. She was still unable to eat or pass stool. Her stomach grew more extensive from the unpassable food, weakening her body.

The head surgeon returned on the third day and said he had no choice but to perform surgery on her. He said he would schedule it for the next week after we did a follow-up visit at his office that Wednesday. In the meantime, I could take her home for the weekend but report to his office on Wednesday for further observations. Mandatory surgery would be performed if the intestines were still twisted and the bowel blocked.

He gave me some bottles of enema and instructed me to use them on her to loosen her bowels.

I checked my daughter out of the hospital on Friday and went home on a hope and a prayer. I hoped that God would heal my daughter without surgery. I prayed that God would intervene and untwist her intestines. There was no other help I knew.

It was now Sunday, a church day. I dressed up my daughter and myself, ready to attend church. I got in my car and turned the key in the ignition, but nothing happened. The car would not start. I was puzzled and frustrated. I asked my neighbor if he could help me with my car, but he could not get it to work either.

I called my fiancé, a minister at his church, but he said he knew nothing about cars. And in his defense, he was honestly clueless. He told me to call his best friend, a shade tree mechanic. I called the friend, who answered his phone and promised to come to the house to try fixing the car. It was already 11:30 a.m., half an hour into the church service. I waited, but he did not show up or call back. It was now noon.

I decided to take matters into my own hands. I picked up my daughter and carried her back into the house. I walked to my bedroom with my daughter there beside me. I knelt on the floor and prayed earnestly to God. I asked Him to fix my car and let me attend church with my daughter. I asked Him to bless and protect us from the enemy's attacks. LORD, we need a miracle.

Then I got up and went back to my car. I tried cranking it again, hoping and praying. And it happened! The car started! I had heard people talk about how God could get into the functioning of vehicles. But I paid little attention. But that day and what transpired have made a believer out of me. I put my daughter in her car seat, buckled up, and drove the route to church.

But then I realized it was too late to attend my home church. It was already afternoon, and they would be finishing their service soon. I felt embarrassed to show up so late at church. Then I remembered that there was another church nearby that I could go to. It was a storefront church that had just opened recently. It was led by a woman of God who was a prophetess. She had preached at my home church a few weeks ago, and I was impressed by her ministry. She did not know me or my daughter personally, but I felt comfortable attending her church. Since the sudden idea of visiting her church was so pressing, maybe God wanted me to go there for a reason. So I decided to go to the storefront church and see what God had in store for us. Maybe God was trying to tell me something.

I drove to the storefront church, hoping to catch the service before it ended. I parked my car and got out with my daughter in my arms. The church was a small but lively place, filled with people who loved God and praised Him through dance. I could feel His presence and power as I walked in. I arrived in time to still hear the sermon.

The prophetess stood in the pulpit, ready to deliver God's word. She was a woman of God with a prophecy and healing gift. She visited my home church a few weeks ago, and I was impressed by her ministry. But she did not know me or my daughter personally. She had never met us or talked to us before.

I sat down on a pew near the middle of the church with my daughter on my lap. She suddenly started coughing. It was a dry and harsh cough that made her gasp for air. The prophetess noticed her and walked over to us. She laid her hands on my daughter's head and prayed with power and authority.

Then the Holy Spirit fell upon the prophetess, and she began to give a word of knowledge about my daughter's condition. She spoke by the Holy Spirit and said things that amazed me. Through the Holy Spirit, she knew exactly what was going on with my daughter's health, even though she had never seen her medical records or heard her diagnosis. She knew she had a condition with her stomach and intestines since birth. The prophetess specifically said through the Holy Spirit, "Ever since this child has been born, she has had a problem with her stomach." She knew that the devil was behind it all. "The devil has attacked her" is what the prophetess revealed in the Holy Spirit.

She continued to speak by the Holy Spirit and said that the devil had peeped into my daughter's future. And he knew that she would be a strong missionary in the LORD. The enemy wanted to discourage me, and if he could not do so, he would attack my daughter. He was trying to hinder my daughter's destiny. He had been attacking her since she was in my womb, trying to abort and harm her. The enemy knew my daughter's assignment--that she had a calling to be a prophet of the LORD and to spread His Word through a podcast, a television ministry, and traveling across this world spreading the gospel of Jesus.

God knows our future, but the devil can sense our purpose and assignment. He knows when we were born and what circumstances surrounded our birth. The enemy knows what gifts and talents we have and what potential we have in Christ. He knows what we can do for God's Kingdom if we follow His will and ways. That's why he attacks us. He is trying to stop us from fulfilling our purpose and assignment. We are a threat to the devil and his kingdom. "For we wrestle not against flesh and blood, but against principalities, against powers, against the rulers of the darkness of this world, against spiritual wickedness in high places." (Ephesians 6:12)

The prophetess gave examples of people from the Bible the devil attacked from birth because they had a special calling from God. She mentioned Moses, who was born in Egypt when Pharaoh ordered all the Hebrew baby boys to be killed because he feared one of them would be a deliverer for God's people (Exodus 1:15-22). She mentioned John the Baptist, who was filled with the Holy Spirit even before he was born and leaped in his mother's womb when he sensed the presence of Jesus in Mary's womb (Luke 1:41-44). He was born to prepare the way for Jesus, the Messiah, the world's Savior.

The prophetess then rebuked the foul spirit of the enemy tormenting my daughter and commanded him to take his filthy hands off her bowels. She prophesized that God was healing her of this condition and that she would not need surgery. She said, "I will not say that she will never have to go to a hospital again, but God said - for this - no surgery."

The following week after the prophecy, I took my daughter to the follow-up visit with the head surgeon that Wednesday. His office was on Eastmoreland Avenue in downtown Memphis. He took X-rays of my daughter's stomach area and asked us to wait in the waiting room until he got the results.

The doctor came back soon, but he looked stunned and confused. He had the X-ray films in his hands, staring at them as if he couldn't believe what he saw. He walked over to me and said tremblingly that the intestines had been untwisted and were no longer blocked. Still looking stunned and his eyes still staring at the results on the X-ray, he announced that my daughter did NOT need surgery. No surgery!

God confirmed His word through the prophetess and rebuked the devil. God healed my daughter. I thank Him for His healing power and His faithfulness. He showed His love and mercy to us.

Everything was connected to her born day, even the enemy's attacks. The enemy knew when she was born; she had purpose and destiny in God's plan.

The enemy tried but failed to take her out of life and hinder her destiny. God protected her and preserved her for His glory. She is now a great spokesperson for God's Kingdom and has a podcast where she uplifts other believers.

We are all great in God's eyes. Our God and even the devil, our enemy, know this. Now, if the enemy knows our greatness isn't it more meaningful and urgent that we know who we are and our worth in God?

That's why we must get acquainted with our purpose and embrace our birthday. We need to ask God what He wants us to do with our lives, what gifts and talents He has given us, and what mission and calling He has for us. We need to seek His guidance and direction in everything we do.

My born day is December 25; I share this date with the celebration of Jesus Christ's birth. The word Christmas comes from the Mass of Christ, which means the celebration of Christ. I am honored and humbled to be born on this day when we remember and rejoice over the greatest gift that God ever gave us - His Son, Jesus, our Lord, and Savior. It is a day when I feel the most blessed and grateful for all God has done for me. It is also a day when I often face attacks from the enemy because it is Christmas Day - when we honor and worship Christ.

I am not saying that my birthday is more important than others. No, it does not mean that at all. All birthdays are important and special to God. He created each of us with love and care and knew every detail about us (Psalm 139:13-16). He has a plan and a purpose for each of us (Jeremiah 29:11). He loves each one of us with an everlasting love (Jeremiah 31:3). Pray and seek God for the significance of your birthday and what you were born to do.

Finally, if you are born again of the Spirit of God, this is a second opportunity to know and seek what you were born to do. This is a new birth, life, and creation in Christ (John 3:3-8; 2 Corinthians 5:17). This is a chance to start over, live for God's glory, and follow His will (Romans 12:1-2). Ask God, and do not copy someone else's ministry or spiritual calling. There is no time for envy or jealousy. You are given a second chance to know and do what you were born to do - BORN DAY!

CHAPTER 3

৩৩৩

Not Even a Hat

"But as for you, ye thought evil against me; but God meant it unto good...."

THE SCRIPTURE IS taken from Genesis 50:20. It is part of Joseph's speech to his brothers when they asked for forgiveness after their father, Jacob, died. Joseph reassured them that he did not hold any grudge against them for selling him into slavery because God used their evil acts and turned them around for good to save many. What is meant to harm you will only excel you.

Joseph recognized that God was sovereign over his life and that he had a plan to use him for good, even when he faced hardship and injustice. This verse shows God's grace and providence in the lives of his people. What is meant to harm you will only excel you.

Even though I spent many hours by my birth mother's bedside before she passed away, her children turned their backs on me as soon as she was gone. They were my biological siblings, but they acted like I was a stranger.

They reminded me of Jephthah, the outcast son in the Book of Judges, who was rejected by his half-brothers and denied his share of the family inheritance. The irony was that we were not entirely blood-related—only me and a younger brother. I don't say this to dishonor or betray my brothers and sisters. I love them dearly. I want to expose the hypocrisy and wickedness of their plan. For further reading, you can find the history and story of Jephthah in the book of Judges, chapters 11-12.

But despite their evil intentions, harsh treatment, and indifference, the LORD orchestrated a blessing for me beyond measure. He arranged a special gift for me. My birth mother's spirit was behind this gift for her daughter. I have this conviction based on the following reasons from the Bible. The Bible alludes to the fact that after the deceased has transitioned, they are still aware of what is happening.

Consider the story of the rich man and Lazarus in the Bible. The scripture vividly depicts the rich man looking across a great chasm and seeing Lazarus resting in Abraham's arms. The rich man had a clear vision of another realm. In the Gospel of Luke, Jesus shares this parable about Lazarus and the rich man. It reveals the relationship between life and death.

Next, the author of Hebrews also tells us that we are surrounded by a cloud of witnesses who have gone before us. These witnesses are the ones who have finished their race and entered Heaven. But they are not indifferent to us. They can see and cheer for us as we run our race on this journey called life. "Therefore, since such a great cloud of witnesses surrounds us, let us throw off everything that hinders and the sin that so easily entangles, and let us run with perseverance the race marked out for us."—Hebrews 12:1

Finally, the Bible reveals that the martyrs in Heaven have a clear view of what is happening on Earth. In Revelation 6:10-11, they cry out for God's justice and receive white robes. The martyrs in Revelation were killed because of their faith in Jesus Christ. They had not forgotten what happened to them and asked God when their lives would be avenged. God gives them a white robe and tells them to wait for a particular task.

When my biological mother made it to Heaven, she could see a bit clearer now. She remembered her suffering, and she could also see the injustice suffered by her daughter imposed by her other children. She cried! LORD, avenge the suffering. And she was met with the reply, "You got a special task to do."

When Mrs. Dorothy Mae transitioned to Heaven, she made peace with hatred, bitterness, jealousy, and quilt—because these unrighteous thoughts and deeds cannot enter the Kingdom of God. She made peace, and she could see things more clearly now. I believe, for the first time, she could truly see me—her daughter.

Mrs. Dorothy Mae now understood why I refused to hate the woman who loved her child and raised me, even though she tried to persuade me otherwise. God is love. Love for everyone is a reality on Earth and in Heaven. "LORD, let your Will be done on Earth as it is in Heaven." God's very nature and essence is love. Oh, Mrs. Dorothy Mae can see more precisely now.

Mrs. Dorothy Mae can now see why I never called the woman who loved and raised her child a stepmother. A woman who sacrificially loves and raises another woman's child as her own is not just a stepmother—she is a mother. God loves us unconditionally and with sacrificial love. He calls us to love him and others as he loves us. God is love and wants us to know and share his passion. There is nothing or nobody closer to compare with God's love—than a mother's love.

Oh, Mrs. Dorothy Mae sees now.

There is an old classic song written by Johnny Nash, and the recorded lyrics are:

> *I can see clearly now the rain is gone*
> *I can see all obstacles in my way*
> *Gone are the dark clouds that had me blind*
> *It's gonna be a bright (bright)*
> *Bright (bright) sunshiny day*

Nobody but a God can open blind eyes and turn hopeless and unsurmountable situations around—But God!

No one can derail God's plans or promises with their mistakes or sins. God is at work with *all* things. This not only helps us forgive those who repent of their conduct and actions, but it also helps us to let go and move on with our lives without any regrets or remorse. And we know everything works together for the good (Romans 8:28).

CHAPTER **4**

The Devil Won't Be Able To Stop This "A Special Task"

OD'S HAND AT work is a message that runs throughout the Bible and history. God is not a distant or passive observer of his creation. He is actively involved in every detail and circumstance. He works out his purposes and plans for his glory and our good. He guides, protects, provides, corrects, and blesses his people. He uses ordinary people and extraordinary events to accomplish his will. He reveals his power, wisdom, and love in everything he does. God's hand at work is a message that inspires us to trust him.

We are not ignorant of the devil's devices. The Bible says he goes around like a roaring lion seeking whom he may devour. But

I write to remind you that the devil is toothless. He is a toothless roaring lion—a bully roaring with no bite. I want to remind and illustrate to you that the devil may try to hinder, harm, or deceive us, but he cannot stop God's plan and power. The devil is a defeated foe. We have the promise and the presence of God to sustain us. We have the Word and the Spirit of God to guide us. We have the name and the blood of Jesus to protect us. Devil, you won't be able to stop us. This chapter's message challenges us to stand firm and overcome any obstacle by faith. God got us—But God!

Even though my brothers and sisters had a particular disposition toward me, God began to operate in direct opposition against their ill wills. He had a plan, and I could see it unfolding in how things began orchestrating in my life after my birth mother's death. There was a pattern and a meaning behind every event and circumstance. It was God's hand at work.

The day after my birth mother's funeral and burial, my daughter woke me up and told me about an unusual event she had the previous evening. She informed me that her grandmother had come to visit her and was sitting at the foot of her bed, smiling warmly. Despite not wanting the same sighting for myself, I accepted my daughter's account of the events. But immediately, I prayed, "God, please do not let me see anything." Not a spirit. Not a ghost. Not anything at all. God, "I am OK." I did not want to see any sightings. I do not want to see anything if it is not walking alive. Well, this request was answered, at least for now.

As fate would have it, I had been working as a teacher with middle school students who needed extra enrichment. The summer school program was coming to an end. We celebrated their progress by taking them to a fun place in Collierville, Tennessee. It was a skating rink called Funquest. It had a large floor for roller skating, a snack bar, and arcade machines. The students were excited to go and have some fun on wheels skating. Once the trip was approved, we crammed the eager kids onto the large, yellow school bus. Since one of the teachers lived in Mississippi and would have to ride thirty miles back to the school after chaperoning the skating event, he quickly decided to drive his car. The rink site was closer to his house.

As you will see, God was in the plan for this man to make this decision. It shows how God orchestras events and orders every detail to carry out His Will for us. God is in control, and nothing happens by coincidence.

Although the middle school teachers selected the venue for this celebratory activity, most bus passengers were young elementary school-age kids. As the bus drove along the winding road of a rural area of Fayette County, the children's excitement grew louder and louder. They pressed their faces against the windows, eager to catch a glimpse of their destination. The middle school teachers had chosen a special place for their end-of-year celebration, but most students were from the adjacent elementary school. The bus was filled with laughter, chatter, and anticipation as they approached the skating rink.

Once we arrived and entered the building, the skating rink was dazzling, with colorful lights and upbeat music. But as the students strapped on their skates, a wave of anxiety swept the young elementary kids. Most had never skated before and felt wobbly and unsteady on their feet. The wooden floor looked like a slippery trap, waiting to make them fall and hurt themselves. They clung to the walls and the benches, too scared to venture onto the rink.

To inspire the timid youngsters, I strapped on a pair of skates myself, thinking, "If they see this old lady teacher gliding on the floor like a smooth butterfly, this will spark their curiosity and courage to try skating." Surely, if this old lady educator can do it, so can they. Not that I am so old, but to young children, anyone over forty is ancient.

I was confident in my decision because I grew up skating on adjustable metal roller skates with a brown leather strap over my shoes. I grew up in the hood, where most African-American children skated in streets in the hood. The hood is a slang term for a neighborhood where people sharing a similar ethnic or racial background live. I use the word hood to express pride or solidarity with my community. Of course, we had to go in the house when the street post lights came on. Our mamas did not play about us roaming the streets at night.

Skating in the 70s era for African-Americans was one of our favorite leisure activities. From skating in the streets, I advanced to owning a pair of professional white roller skates ordered and purchased from Sears and Roebuck's store catalog. I decked the roller skates out with colorful fluffy balls and silver bells attached and spent many weekends skate-dancing to disco music, P-Funks tracks song by Sly and the Family Stone, Jimi Hendrix, and the Parliament-Funkadelic. Black rolling skating rinks were a global phenomenon.

I was a master of skating backward, doing the split like James Brown while zipping across the rink; I was bunny-hopping on my roller, too. This boosted my confidence even more to encourage the young children. I had some excellent skills on the floor, which made what happened next even more baffling. It had to be God's hand at work. Ain't nobody God but God—He is the master plan.

The Hokey-Pokey song blasted from the rink's speakers. It was a loud and unmistakable time to get on the floor, have fun, and, most importantly, show your skills.

You put your right foot in.
You take your right foot out and skate in all about.
You put your left foot in.
You take your left foot out and skate in all about.
You put your whole self in.
You take your whole self out.
And turn it all around.

As the song went on, I felt a surge of energy in my body. But when I put my right foot in this time, it flew up like a rocket, taking my whole body with it.

I don't know how long I hung in the air. It felt like an eternity. The only thing I could see was my birth mother's face. It filled the entire ceiling of the skating arena, blocking everything else from my sight. She smiled at me warmly, and I heard her voice in my spirit, even though her lips didn't move. "Everything is going to be OK." She appeared and was there for a *particular task.*

49

It was like a soft voice caressing my soul—a loving heart reaching out to a longing heart that craved to hear those words. Words I longed to hear from her when she walked this Earth. As the words filled my spirit, my heart overflowed. As her face faded from the arena, I knew I had no choice but to fall on the hard wooden skating floor. Bang!

I was wearing a wig that day and dreaded the idea of it flying off my head and exposing my 'pigtails' to everyone. Not just one or two pigtails, but many scattered over my head. It was a horrifying thought. Vanity, vanity, why I was concerned about a wig and how my hair looks, I thought later.

Caught up in vanity, I quickly decided to fall for some cuteness. With this decision, I landed on my right hand and snapped my wrist—bearing the total weight of my body. I crashed on the floor. But at least that wig was still on my head. Vanity!

After the humiliating fall, but with that wig still on my head, I attempted to use my hands to lift myself from the floor. My right hand was motionless, and the pain was rushing from the tip of my fingers through my entire right arm. My right hand and wrist were twitching on my body like a fish fresh out of water.

The hand was so swollen that it ballooned like a hot air balloon. The wrist was twisted in a physically distorted position. I was shocked as my swollen hand and wrist moved and jerked uncontrollably. My hand and wrist went into their own personal shock. They were having a moment on their own. I could no longer control the distorted movements.

Was God's hand in this? It all seemed like at that moment it was hand. My hand was in a mess—trauma. But someone said, "When you get in trouble, He steps right in."

Two female teachers who helped chaperone the trip started mocking the situation. "She should have known better than to drag her old tail out on that floor." "When you are old, your bones don't heal like when you were young." "She had no business putting her old self on those skates."

But I encouraged myself that the decision was for the children's sake, not for me. Sometimes you just got to encourage yourself. I thought about David's words from the Bible, "I was young, but now I am old, and I have never seen the righteous forsaken...."—Psalm 37:25

At this point, I was sure God had not abandoned me or these old bones. The lesson learned was to watch out for whose presence you fall because not everyone is a friend. Some associates are fake and shady—frenemies.

The male teacher, the only one who drove his car that day, picked me up from the floor and sped me to the emergency room at Baptist Hospital in Collierville. We see how God arranges people, things, and events—this was the only person who abruptly chose to drive his vehicle that day. This was not a random chance. God's hand was in it from the beginning.

When we got to the emergency room, I was in agony. I couldn't walk. The fall had broken my wrist. My wrist was broken, but my whole body was in shock from the pain. A wheelchair was brought to the car, and I was wheeled to the admission counter of the emergency room. The receptionist took my information and asked for my insurance. I felt embarrassed because I didn't have medical insurance. I worked for a rural school district, where teachers' base salary was one of the lowest and worst in the state.

I didn't want anyone to know that I didn't have medical insurance. How stupid, I thought. Who goes without insurance? What am I going to do now? The only thing I could think of was to hide my embarrassment, and I did so by using an emotional deflector. I sobbed louder and louder to distract myself from my humiliation.

That was when the male teacher who drove his car to the skating rink that day spoke up out of the blue. He quickly told the emergency receptionist, "This is Workers' Comp." There I was, sitting in the wheelchair with my wrist dangling from my arm and my finger swollen, big crocodile tears streaming down my face, nose, and mouth. I did not know about workers' compensation or what the term meant. But this man knew. He knew exactly what to say and do. He said that since I had injured my wrist on a school trip, I qualified for medical care and treatment for my wrist and that the receptionist should write on the intake form—Workers' Comp.

My tears began to dry, and I was wheeled back to a medical procedure room in the emergency room. Two medical doctors entered the room where I was lying in the emergency room bed. They looked at my wrist and said it was a "doozy."

My wrist was severely broken in two places, and I would need surgery. I went into shock again and almost shook off the bed at the sound of the word--surgery. One doctor was so kind and attentive that he politely held my legs still so I wouldn't fall out of bed and damage my already broken wrist more. I am now crying because I dread needles and operations.

The other doctor excused himself from the room. Seeing my overwhelming trepidation with the thought of undergoing surgery, the remaining doctor assured me he would not perform surgery on the broken wrist. Still, I needed to make an appointment and report to Campbell Clinic Orthopedics to evaluate my wrist and the extent of the injury sustained.

The doctor proceeded to secure no further damages to the broken wrist. He wrapped my wrist by putting a bandage on the inside of the wrist and wrapped it around my arm until it reached my elbow. He repeated the procedure and wrapped my broken wrist twice. After dressing and securing my wrist, I was discharged from the emergency room with written instructions to contact and make an immediate appointment with Campbell Clinic.

The male teacher who drove me to the emergency drove me to pick up my car. I then went home with him trailing my vehicle to ensure I made it home safely since I could only operate the car at 20 mph. And trying to steer with my left hand was almost impossible. I desperately tried to maintain the road and drive with my left hand.

Upon my arrival home, I thanked this man. I told him I was grateful for him being my spokesperson by advising the emergency room to file the injury under Workers' Compensation. I so appreciated this man and knew he was a godsend. God's hand was in the plan.

However, only some people at the school were supportive. The personnel director, who was in charge of handling workers' compensation claims, was very hostile and unprofessional. She called me the following Monday and demanded that I return the classroom key. She said she needed it to close out the equipment requisitioned for summer school. I told her I still had the key but couldn't drive thirty miles to the district office to bring it to her. I asked her how she expected me to do that when my right wrist hung from my arm. She was furious. She tried to insinuate that I was exaggerating the seriousness of my injury. Then in an outburst of anger, she shouted, "Who told you to file your injury under Workers' Compensation?" She threatened to deny the claim and hold my summer payroll check. "The devil is a liar," I thought to myself. I was shocked by her words. I couldn't believe she, the personnel director at the district's central office, could be rude and unprofessional. She added insult to injury.

Her rude tone and denial to release my payroll check prompted me to seek legal advice. I called a labor relations attorney to ask if it was lawful for an employer to hold an employee's paycheck for hours worked. I also told the attorney why the personnel director threatened to do so. This prompted a conversation about the injury to my wrist from the school's excursion to the skating rink. The labor relations attorney stopped me abruptly and stated, "You are worried about the wrong thing." "The employer cannot hold your paycheck—it is unlawful." "You will get your check, "but you have a legally binding workers' compensation case against your employer.

I only knew a little about workers' compensation, with most of the information learned from the man who took me to the emergency room. But I was glad to know I had a case. The attorney explained that it was a program that provided benefits to employees who were injured on the job. He said that it would cover my medical bills and lost wages. He noted that it was a legal right and a moral duty for the school to compensate me for my injury.

The attorney insisted that I allow him to file a workers' compensation case against the employer for the severity of the damage to my wrist. After carefully listening and recalling the harsh and disrespectful outburst of the personnel director, I readily agreed with the attorney. I retained the attorney, and he filed a legal lawsuit against the employer for damages to my wrist.

I remained in the care of Campbell Clinic for treatment of my broken wrist for almost a year. They put a long cast on my arm, reaching my right elbow, and told me to keep it elevated and dry. I once had a panic attack with that cast restricting my arm and movement. I hate to feel caged in; it goes for any part of my body. I felt like I was suffocating. Like Maya Angelou, I also know why the caged bird sings.

My orthopedic doctor said I would have to wear the cast for six weeks and then return for a check-up and physical therapy. The break to my wrist was so severe and complicated that I had to wear a second cast at the end of six weeks. This cast was a bit shorter and stopped mid-way at the forearm. They also gave me some exercises at home to keep my fingers and elbow flexible. My house looked like a gym with all the medical equipment shipped to my home from Campbell Clinic.

The wrist was taking a considerable time to heal correctly, and I lost all functions of my right hand and fingers. I needed surgery as the previous doctor suggested at Baptist Hospital in Collierville. However, I was skeptical about being cut on for surgery. And the attending orthopedic doctor was too nervous about a malpractice lawsuit because Campbell Clinic knew I was under the watchful eye of an attorney regarding every procedure. Therefore, I had a long healing process and had to learn, with the help of intense physical therapy to learn how to use my wrist and right hand again.

There was a disconnect in my brain and a realization that I had a right hand. I understand when a wounded veteran loses a limb, and the brain thinks that the limb is still there, and the veteran experiences pain stemming from the brain as if the severed limb was still attached to the body. My experiences were similar as it relates to the brain. My right hand was still attached to my body, but my brain was not receiving the signal, nor was my brain sending a signal to the hand. I could not move my right hand or my fingers. The episode was odd and scary.

Faced with this oddity, I began to pray and seek God for healing. I attended a revival at a local church where I knew a well-known national and television evangelist was preaching and praying for those needing healing. I arrived at the revival with my right hand concealed in a special glove designed by Campbell Clinic. The glove was made out of a stretchy nude fabric. The nude color of the glove did not blend well with my African-American melanin skin tone. At the end of each finger insert of the glove were rubber bands to pull and attach to a central spot on the glove to assert pressure on my hand in an attempt to flex my fingers to force them to move. I looked like Edward Scissorhands minus the scissors but with rubber bands instead.

The evangelist called for a prayer line for all those needing God's healing grace. I entered the healing line. When it eventually reached my time to stand in front of the evangelist to ask for prayer personally. The evangelist was human. He looked at the rubber band, Edward Scissorhands glove strangely. After he got over his initial thought of wondering what type of odd-looking apparatus is this, he asked if I could remove the glove. I nodded, "Yes."

When I removed the glove, he rubbed holy anointing oil in the palm of my hand and prayed for healing. Then, something unexpected happened—the evangelist began to prophesy.

The evangelist started to prophesy these words over my life, "This happened for a reason." "The LORD allowed this to happen." The LORD said, "He is getting ready to bless you financially through this hand." Then the evangelist began to pat my hand. Now, I wonder if he forgot I was coming up for healing because why is he patting on a wounded hand? I thank God that He does not look at our short-sightedness and human fragility with contempt as He is trying to bless us. God's thoughts are higher than ours. His mercy is everlasting. Thank goodness!

I was intently focused on healing, but God's plan for all of this was to bless me substantially. The evangelist ended the prophecy with these words, "God is going to bless you so much money through this hand that you won't be able to count it." It was all a part of God's higher plan.

The last months of the healing process were challenging. I was still under the care of Campbell Clinic, and my hand was slowly progressing. I could move my fingers slightly, but my wrist and hand were still not completely healed. I often felt pain and discomfort, especially when I tried to do simple tasks like writing on the school board while conducting classes at school. When will I be able to use my hand as usual again? My faith was being tested.

In hopes of encouraging words of healing, I got in another prayer line for full recovery of my wrist and right hand. This time it was called by a visiting evangelist conducting a revival at my home church. Strange enough, when I got in line and stood before him, he did not pray for my hand. He began to praise God in a holy dance. He told me he was praising God for me because God was about to bless me financially.

Then enthusiastically announced, *"The devil won't be able to stop this!"* God said, "The devil won't be able to stop this blessing." He took my left hand in his and offered me the invitation to honor God with praise for the money God was preparing to release. I praised the LORD!

It is now ten months after the initial breakage of my wrist. The number ten represents the completion of a cycle. It was the end of my duration and process at Campbell Clinic. All the doctors at the clinic were very professional and helpful, and I appreciated their service. However, something unique happened during my final visit to the clinic.

My attending orthopedic doctor asked if I knew the disability rate he had given me and likewise reported to my attorney. Since I did not fully understand workers' compensation laws, I knew nothing about a disability rating. But for some reason, he needed to disclose this information to me. He was persistent. I listened and thanked him for sharing the information, still trying to figure out the purpose of the disclosure.

After completing my time and cycle with Campbell Clinic, my attorney can file the lawsuit and start ligations. Filing the workers' compensation case took work. My employer tried to deny my claim and blame me for the accident. They said I was negligent and never should have been on the skates if I could not skate. The fact of the matter is I could skate. They also tried to intimidate and pressure me to accept a low settlement. But I did not give up. I knew I had hired a competent and experienced attorney who fought for my rights. He was the person who took the time to explain workers' compensation to me and begged me to allow him to handle the case. I was confident I had a strong chance of winning if we filed a lawsuit against the employer.

After filing with the court, a notice of the lawsuit was sent to the employer. The personnel director was back to her old tricks, and she called me and asked me if I would be willing to settle out of court. I politely listened to her proposal and quickly realized she had offered minimal money. "Nope, not for my pain and suffering," I thought, "and all the hell she put me through." She was rude and disrespectful when I initially injured my wrist. She showed me no mercy, and I was not about to show her any mercy in her foolery. I am sticking to the plan—God's plan. No further conversation; I will see you in court with my attorney. I politely hung up the phone.

After filing the case, my attorney soon contacted me and asked me to meet him at his office. He told me the school's attorney wanted to meet with me to conduct a private deposition. A deposition is a formal interview where the opposing party asks you questions under oath. My attorney arranged that I meet with the school's attorney at his law firm, and he prepared me for what to expect. However, during the deposition, the school's attorney asked me an odd question that was supposed to catch me off guard and put the school district at the advantage of the settlement.

He asked me, "What do you think the disability rate is for your wrist?" This was strange because only the attending doctor and lawyer were supposed to know this information before trial and litigation. He knew this but thought he could play on my lack of understanding of legal matters.

With this question, he threw out his trump card, resting in his bet that I would throw out a low number like 5 or 6 in my verbal response to his question. But what he did know was that I was holding the "Big Joker." The highest card in the deck when playing a card game of spades. Some people play checkers, but I play chess.

He wanted to meet privately to trap me into revealing something that could hurt my case. He was sure I would answer with a low number for the disability. But God had already prepared me with the answer.

I remembered the persistence of my attending orthopedic doctor during my follow-up and final visit to Campbell Clinic. He was persistent in sharing with me the disability rate he had given on the usage and function of my right hand. I later discovered that the highest disability rate you can provide a patient for a broken wrist is 9%.

This orthopedic doctor gave me a disability rating of 32%. Who does this? No one but God. God can bless us exceedingly and abundantly. The king's heart is in God's hand, as is a doctor's.

As a result, I confidently answered the school's attorney's question with an answer of a 30% disability rate. I did not want to give the actual number; it would have drawn suspicions that someone had disclosed the sealed information. I saw this shyster's face drop in disbelief. He realized he could not win this case, and the settlement would be huge.

The day of the arbitration for the workers' compensation case against the school district finally came. I sat at the table with my attorney, facing the personnel director and their shady lawyer. The arbitrator started the hearing and listened to both sides present their arguments and evidence. The main issue was the disability rate for my injured wrist, which I had hurt during the school outing. Everyone agreed, but the award amount depended on— the disability rate.

The personnel director talked first, and their lawyer tried to lowball me with a ridiculous offer, hoping I would settle. But I stood firm. I remembered all the pain and trouble I had gone through to get to this point. I firmly said "No" to their insulting offer.

My attorney countered with a strong argument, pointing out the high disability rate my orthopedic doctor gave me for my right wrist. This was my dominant hand, and the injury had severely affected it. He also mentioned that my doctor was from Campbell Clinic, one of the best orthopedic clinics in the country. No one could question their expertise or credibility because they wrote the book on orthopedics.

The other side realized they had no chance of winning. God had been on my side from the start, even before I went to the skating rink that fateful day. When the odds seem bad, God can turn it around for our good.

The arbitrator made the decision based on the facts of the case and my acceptance of an award and then announced the amount of the award settlement. The prophets were true prophets of God because *every* word they spoke came to pass. "God said there will be so much money you will not be able to count it in your right hand." I am truly thanking God for his Word, provision, and blessings.

God is sovereign over timing—the seemingly insignificant detail of the school teacher driving his car to the skating rink was right on time and ordained by God, even the timing of the personnel director's rude behavior and refusal to give me my payroll check after I broke my wrist. It was all part of God's plan and timing after I broke my wrist because if the personnel director had not been so stubborn and unprofessional, I would not have needed to contact a lawyer–it all worked out for God's purpose of a blessing for me. God can turn others' evil intentions and actions into tools for His will, making them serve His ultimate goal. This gives us such everlasting peace–that nothing can thwart His plan and that He's involved in every second of our lives. David says, "My times are in your hand" (Psalm 31:15). God holds every moment.

Finally, in some supernatural way, my biological mother had something to do with this blessing. As I fell and flipped into the air at the skating rink and knew a hard landing was inevitable, I saw her face completely covering the circumference of the ceiling, smiling to calm me before I fell. She was on a 'special task.'

She spoke to my spirit and said, "Everything is going to be OK." Those were the words I had longed to hear from her mouth ever since the time we reunited here on Earth. I felt a surge of peace and love in my heart—knowing it would be OK. At the end of all this, you shall see glory.

That all the Earth's people might know the hand of LORD, that it is mighty—Joshua 4:24.

CHAPTER 5

૭૦૭૭

The Cross and the Switchblade: The Grandmother Whom I Never Met

*M*RS. LUCILLE, MY biological grandmother, whom I had never met, was a beautiful woman with thin, wavy hair and sharp features. She had a smooth fair complexion. At that time, this was a "golden ticket" for African-American women, giving them access to certain privileges others did not have.

Mrs. Lucille had a reputation for being fierce and ruthless. Despite her petite and gorgeous appearance, she earned the nickname 'The Cutter' in the family. Mrs. Lucille always carried a mean switchblade and quickly pulled it out if anyone crossed her path in a way that "ticked" her off. One of the stories I heard was how she sliced into the seersucker jacket of a life insurance man who came banging on her door.

The life insurance salesman, a white man, banged on the door to collect a late payment. He was angry about the lateness of her pay on the policy. She told her oldest grandson to answer the door and say, "She is not here." He was not to let the insurance man in the house.

The insurance man peered through the door and saw two feet behind the curtains. He said to the boy, "If your grandmother is not here, then why do I see a pair of female shoes with a foot in each shoe behind the curtains?" "Who is that boy hiding behind that curtain?" He tried to push his way in, but the young boy blocked him. Mrs. Lucille, furious and "ticked" off, sprang from behind the curtains with her switchblade in her hand. She slashed at the white man's seersucker jacket, making him yelp and jump off the porch. He ran down the walkway to his car, leaving a trail of shredded fabric behind him.

Mrs. Lucille hid from the police for over a week after that incident. Then she left town and moved to Chicago, Illinois, with her switchblade. There, something unique happened. By divine intervention, Mrs. Lucille changed her ways and became a Christian. She dedicated her life to church service and joined the usher board.

I never knew her personally, but I heard many interesting stories about her. I admire and respect her for turning her life around and becoming a victor in Christ. It doesn't matter how we start but how we finish. Mrs. Lucille's story is a classic example of what Christ can do in the life of anyone. I honor and respect her legacy as the grandmother I never met. But I would have loved to meet.

❧

Stopping and Understanding Generational Patterns

We are all connected in this vast human family. As John Donne wrote, "No man is an island entire of itself; every man is a piece of the continent." Therefore, we need to understand ourselves as individuals and as members of the family, nation, and race we belong to. This is a vital aspect of self-awareness. We should also acknowledge that we share our family's faults and virtues and are responsible for healing and uplifting our family. As the Bible says, "Bear one another's burdens, and so fulfill the law of Christ." (Galatians 6:2)

SOME FAMILIES STRUGGLE with negative patterns, tendencies, and behaviors that repeat themselves across generations. These are called generational curses, which can cause much pain and problems for the people who inherit them. Generational curses can appear as cycles of dysfunction, addiction, poverty, abuse, or any other situation that robs us of our purpose and destiny. If we want to break free from these curses and live in God's blessing, we must understand where they come from and how they affect us.

We need to learn from the mistakes and successes of our ancestors and choose to follow God's ways. God loves us and has a beautiful plan for our life, and He does not want anything to hinder or derail us. The Bible warns us that people perish for the lack of knowledge. Therefore, knowing and understanding generational patterns is necessary to stop unhealthy ones from interfering with our destiny. Again, we can learn from the good and the bad in our family.

Some families are trapped in negative patterns that span generations. As stated, these patterns can harm their lives, such as addiction, abuse, and poverty—to name a few. But these patterns can be broken with awareness and determination. It may not be easy, but it is possible. Breaking free can be a daunting challenge. No one-size-fits-all solution exists; I don't pretend to know the answer. But I want to offer a spiritual truth that I find helpful.

As the saying goes, "Jesus is the habit breaker." Sin invaded the world through one man and through one man—Jesus—sin was conquered.

Jesus faced the devil's temptations and overcame them. The cycle was broken. Jesus resisted. The Bible tells us to resist the devil, and he will flee from us. Don't drink that third glass of alcohol when feeling tipsy. The first time they hit you, consider leaving or seek professional couples counseling. Don't let it become a second, then a third time because it becomes toxic and abusive. Resist the temptation to stay in an abusive relationship.

By Jesus standing firm and resisting—we are all liberated from the chaining effect of sin through Christ. The same applies to our family; if one person begins to resist the temptations of unhealthy generational patterns, this creates a new possibility for future generations—our children and their children—their freedom and blessing. It only takes that one family member to resist the devil's wiles. It only takes that one person to break the habit. The cycle is broken. All can be free. It is a ripple effect.

As mentioned, not all generational patterns are negative. Some families inherit positive qualities they pass on to their offspring, such as diligence and perseverance. These qualities can help us face difficulties and pursue our dreams. I can attest to this from my diligence in talking with family historians and attending a reunion.

History has it that over the years, the Bennett family shared a journey from the muddy waters of Mississippi to the Pacific Ocean, guided by their unshakeable belief in God. These efforts have afforded them the resources to prosper and become beautiful and gracious people.

The Bennett family has very successful family members: lawyers, doctors, politicians, nurses, educators, preachers, pastors, chefs, daycare owners, realtors, business people, and entrepreneurs. They are a blessed family, individually and collectively.

I was told that my great-great-grandfather Will 'Papa' Bennett went into the field one day and struck a mason jar of money buried in a shallow hole while chopping cotton. That was God's grace. This newly found fortune allowed 'Papa' Bennett to relocate to Chicago, Illinois, and to send the rest of the money back to Batesville and move his family off the plantation.

This miraculous legacy reveals that God has always been with the Bennett Family. He has performed miraculous deeds—no matter the heavy burdens and unhealthy patterns we have had to overcome as a family unit. God has a plan and a purpose for the Bennett Family—individually and collectively.

CHAPTER 7

༄ঌঌঌ৺

A Beloved Father

"The heart of a father is the masterpiece of nature." – Antoine Francois Prevost

*M*Y LIFE WAS divinely shaped by a prophecy that a missionary spoke over me while I was in my biological mother's womb when she attended a prayer meeting at the Pentecostal Temple of COGIC in Memphis, Tennessee. The missionary said that God had a plan for me and that I would be set apart from my siblings. *"When this happened," not if."* My father took me to live in his home with him. I was separated or set apart from the rest of my biological family.

I certainly was not any better than my siblings; I was the youngest at the time and perhaps the least of the bunch. God's setting apart was not based on my merit or superiority but on his sovereign grace. God knows and sees the heart of all of us and fulfills His Word and promise. Ultimately, my father's decision to take me from my biological mother's home and rear me was God's purpose and plan set in motion. And who can argue with God? His ways and thoughts are much higher than ours (Isaiah 55:8).

God's Word is true. It shall not return void, but it shall accomplish that which God purpose, and shall succeed in the thing for which He sent it (Isaiah 55:11).

For I know the plans I have for you," declares the Lord, "plans to prosper you and not to harm you, plans to give you hope and a future (Jeremiah 29:11).

God's Word is true. It shall not return void, but it shall accomplish that which God purpose, and shall succeed in the thing for which He sent it."--Isaiah 55:11

My father, Darnell Fields, cherished me as his firstborn child, baby girl, and only daughter. I was born when he was forty-five years old. Most men would have already fathered a child or children by age twenty or thirty during this time. Just like Joseph was to Jacob, I was born during my father's aged years.

My father worked as a Goldsmith's Department Store truck driver and eventually moved on from Goldsmith's to work at Shriner's School as a driver. In my early years, riding with him in the Goldsmith's truck was one of my favorite activities. He called me "little one," a sweet and endearing nickname that only he could use instead of my real name. He loved the name, Darnella because it was a tribute and the feminine version of his own. And he insisted that everyone use my full name, not a shortened version. I was his little girl, his legacy and namesake.

To this day, I follow this tradition. I do not have a nickname nor allow anyone to call me by a name other than my actual name, Darnella. I tell them I was named after my father, which is my endearing way to honor his legacy. "A good name is to be chosen rather than great riches, loving favor rather than silver and gold."—Proverbs 22:1

My dad was the first man who loved me unconditionally. He taught me how to be confident, assertive, and independent. He showed me how to trust and respect myself and others. He was always there for me, cheering me on, supporting, and protecting me. He never compromised his love for his daughter because he knew how important it was for me to have a positive role model as a father.

A woman can learn much from her father about choosing a partner who will treat her well and appreciate her for who she is. She wants a partner who will love her like her father does.

I never got a whooping from my dad. He only spanked me once with three gentle taps of his hand. The taps didn't hurt at all. My pride was hurt because my dad spanked me. I threw myself on the floor and had a big tantrum. I never received another spanking. I think the entire episode hurt his feeling more than mine. He adored his daughter.

I cherish my dad's loving commitment to taking me under his wings and raising me in his home's stability.

Darnell Fields was not only my dad but also my friend and mentor. My dad followed the rhythm of the farm animals. This is an old expression meaning that he slept early and rose early before dawn. I never saw him skip a day from work. As an honorary gesture, his name is engraved on a plaque on the walls of the Memphis Shelby Board of Education. He was a devoted and diligent worker and compassionately and skillfully worked with children with disabilities at the Shriners School.

To me, he was a wonderful father. My father was my strong tower, always shielding and protecting me. I never had to want anything. All I needed to say was "Daddy" in that little dad-girl voice. You will see a grown man's heart melt.

Just as my father cherished me, I adored him, too. I appreciate that he opened his heart and stood bravely to rescue and raise his child. More so, was it a rescue or just God's Will? It was God's Will. I remembered the words of the prophecy and knew all was at work in God's due timing and season.

God's divine guidance in our life and faith help shape our journey. The Bible says, "Trust in the Lord with all your heart and lean not on your understanding; in all your ways acknowledge him, and he will make your paths straight."—Proverbs 3:5-6.

God's providence is impeccable. He cares and makes provisions for his creation. He provides for our needs and uses others to bless, shield, and protect us. God's providence led my father to care for me and raise me in his home. God's providence in my father's home led me to specific opportunities I probably would not have been afforded if I had lived in another house. The Bible declares in Romans 8:28: "And we know that in all things God works for the good of those who love him, who have been called according to his purpose."

I end this chapter of my life with the loving memory of my beloved father—Mr. Darnell Fields.

Dad, you were the best father I could ever ask or wish for. You always supported me, encouraged me, and loved me unconditionally. You taught me so much about life; I will always cherish the precious memories. You were not only my father but also my friend and my buckler and shield. You loved playing billiards at the pool hall downtown and were a pool shark. You were a soft-spoken man, but you knew how to hold your own when it came to protecting your daughter. I miss you, but I know you are watching over me from above every step of the way. Thank you for everything you did for me and the bravery and sacrifices you made. You will always be in my heart. I love you, "Daddy."

CHAPTER **8**

My Guardian Angel

"Who needs a fairy godmother when you have a grandma." --Unknown

OD HAS A unique plan for your life and a purpose for your existence. He will arrange everything and everyone in your life to either protect you or help you fulfill your purpose. God is in control of every detail of timing and placement for our benefit.

"For I know the plans I have for you," declares the Lord, "plans to prosper you and not to harm you, plans to give you hope and a future." (Jeremiah 29:11)

"The Lord will fulfill his purpose for me; your steadfast love, O Lord, endures forever." (Psalm 138:8)

My life was not exactly a fairy tale, but I always loved the book of Cinderella. I could relate to Cinderella's happy life with her father and her miserable life after he died. But unlike her, I did not suffer at the hands of a miserably evil stepmother, though everything else was similar—even the part where she had a fairy godmother. My fairy godmother was my grandmother–a blessing with a purpose in my life.

God blessed me with a wonderful grandmother who was a powerful, positive influence in my life through my father's mother-in-law. Her name was Vienna Christian, and she loved me as her only grandchild. She was a woman who showed me grace and planted the seed of virtue in my life that only God could provide. She taught me most of what I know about Christianity and made a massive difference in my life.

"Train up a child in the way he should go; even when he is old he will not depart from it." (Proverbs 22:6)

I still remember the first puzzle she gave me that said, "For God So Loved the World," John 3:16.

She was a faithful Christian, Church Member, and Sunday School Teacher and always behaved like a lady of dignity. She had a soft perfume that lingered in the air when she walked in or out of a room. People loved Mrs. Vienna Christian coming and going. She was affectionately called "Mrs. V" by her family and loved ones. She and my grandfather were business owners and hard-working people. She taught me how to give and serve others in need. I went with her to many places like Foote Homes, Clearborn Homes, and Dixie near downtown Memphis, where she helped feed and provide food to those in need and their families. My grandfather helped run the store, but I am sure he gave additional products to people in need. This was both of their characters. However, my grandmother made it her mission to build up the Kingdom by giving and tending to those in need.

"She opens her hand to the poor and reaches out her hands to the needy." (Proverbs 31:20)

"Whoever is generous to the poor lends to the Lord, and he will repay him for his deed." (Proverbs 19:17)

My grandmother, whom I affectionately called "Big Mama," was wholeheartedly my guardian angel. However, she was unlike the Big Mamas we now see on television. Nope, she was a stylist woman of God full of grace. She was a gracious woman who shielded and protected the fidelity and integrity of her granddaughter.

My grandmother saved me from a dangerous situation just in time. I was permitted to go out of town with some cousins and their families. My family didn't know (or so I thought) that one of the male cousins was a rapist who had his eyes on me. I used to go to his house some days after school because his parents looked after me since they lived close to my school. He would try to touch me inappropriately. I was a young child, but I would push his hand away firmly. I felt uncomfortable and knew something was wrong with his actions. I thought no one else knew what he was doing, and I didn't tell anyone because nothing serious had happened. He only tried to touch me, and I always slapped his hands from around me and stopped him from touching me.

Nothing is more traumatic than being abused by people you trust, especially for the girl child who doesn't understand what is happening to her because of her hormones. The shock and confusion often lead to anger, isolation, and shame. Some girls end up feeling guilty for being abused by pedophiles who use their relationship with the victims to satisfy their desires.

As an insert in this memoir, this behavior can happen in a church where we are around trusted members. Pedophiles often hide in churches where they can use the pulpit and their religion to cover their evil deeds. But young girls or young ladies, if they have abused you, please know that it was not your fault. You were innocent, and they took advantage of you. You are still who God says you are–innocent. You are a precious young girl who wicked people harmed. But your identity and true self lie within God's truth about you. Live in grace and live in freedom.

"A Rose Is Still a Rose" is a song by the late American singer, Aretha Franklin. It was written and produced by singer, Lauryn Hill, for Mrs. Franklin's same name (1998) album. The song is about a woman who advises a younger woman who keeps getting hurt by bad relationships. In "A Rose Is Still a Rose," Mrs.

Franklin tells her that no matter what happens, even though the woman has been "wounded and scarred," the woman is "still a rose."

You are who God says you are--beautifully and wonderfully made.

"He heals the brokenhearted and binds up their wounds." (Psalm 147:3)

"The Lord is near to the brokenhearted and saves the afflicted in spirit." (Psalm 34:18)

In addition to this insert, this can also happen to our young boys and men. Young boys and men do not let the twisted insatiable lust of others determine who you are and your gender. You are who God said you are from the beginning. Your gender and destiny are not predicated sex acts, whether warranted or unwarranted. God stands with His hands stretched out for a repentant soul. God restores.

So, the day came for me to go out of town with this cousin and that same family. I was at the train station with a ticket for my final destination to Chicago, Illinois. My grandmother had a revelation and sensed the peril I would face if I got on that train. I don't know if it was a divine warning or a grandmother's instinct, but she saved me from going on that trip.

My grandmother reached the train station just in time as I was about to board the train and gently grabbed my arm. She had a serious look, and without any doubt or delay, she told that family, "Darnella will not be going on this trip." She calmly walked along the train with me by her side. She never turned back as we left the train station, and I walked beside her with my hand firmly clasped in hers.

That was also the last babysitting job for that family as it relates to my staying at that house after school.

My grandfather (Big Daddy) was also a blessing and kept me safe. I remember him coming to get me from school after the incident of me no longer being allowed to be babysat by that family in his shiny Blue Deuce and Quarter – Buick Electra 225. Those were the fancy cars of the time. My grandparents had two – one for each of them. They were successful business owners and lived a comfortable lifestyle.

I appreciate the grandparents God gave me for their unfailing love, guidance, and protection. We can't choose our family, but God will guide our steps and make way for us to fulfill our destiny and His plan for our lives.

"A man's heart plans his way, but the Lord directs his steps." (Proverbs 16:9)

CHAPTER 9

೪ఴఴౣ

The Demise of Two Generous Souls

"To live in hearts we leave behind is not to die."--Thomas Campbell

*M*Y GUARDIAN ANGEL, my grandmother, is gone! This was the first devastating loss I experienced. My grandmother's death, Mrs. Vienna Christian's "Bigmama," happened during my junior year of high school. She was always my biggest support, and I was devastated because she stood by me when I was nominated to be a Queen or Princess at school. She was my number one fan and supporter. All I had to do was say, "Bigmama," and she would leap into action every time. She indeed had a golden heart.

I was the president of the typing and parliamentarian clubs at school, and they both chose me to run for queen. The contest was based on selling everyday household items, and I recall having calendars to sell. My grandmother, who had a good reputation and influence in Memphis, made some phone calls on my behalf, and I got a lot of sales and money for my campaign.

During the sales campaign, I vividly remember my grand-mother walking into one of the bedrooms of my grandparents' house, clutching her right leg at the calf and groaning that it hurt. She sat for a while in the green velvet cushion chair. After resting in the chair for a while, she got up and resumed walking as usual. We didn't think it was an emergency because she was usually not ill and had no major underlying medical issues. It was the final week of the competition for the school's campaign and the opportunity for her granddaughter to be crowned queen.

On the final day of the fundraiser, my grandmother came to my parent's home to give me the money she had raised for her grandchild. After giving me the money, she did something very unusual. She lay down on my bed.

It was surprising and unusual because she was very particular about keeping bedrooms clean and tidy. And she respected the cleanliness and tidiness of others. She would always say, "Please sit on a chair or a sofa if you need to rest. Please, don't sit on the bed." Beds were meant for sleeping in and not just sitting and flopping your body on--especially with your outside clothes. "Cleanliness is the next best thing to Godliness."

She grabbed her leg while reclining across my bed and began groaning again. She was taken to Baptist Hospital for severe leg pain.

Within a week, my mother received a phone call from my grandfather. He informed her that my grandmother had died from a blood clot in her leg that had traveled to her heart. It was fast and fatal.

My mother and I rushed to the hospital. I kissed my grandmother softly on her cheek, hoping she could feel how much I loved, adored, and appreciated her. She was my only grandmother, and I was her only grandchild. There is no pain like losing a loved one. The loss of my grandmother was my first loss. I was fifteen years old. There was a void, and I was stunned. My God!

The subsequent devasting loss came with losing my father. I was seventeen years old.

My father lived long enough to see me graduate from high school with honors and a four-year college scholarship. I know that God rewarded him this night for his love and faithfulness. My father lived for my education and did everything possible to afford me a good education. God never forgets our labor of love and gives special favors to those who trust him.

Then came the night of our high school graduation party. My best friend, a graduate, said it would be the best party ever. All the cool people would be there, but the party wouldn't start jumping off until around 11:00 p.m. I knew that would be a problem for my parents. My curfew was midnight.

My friend was so excited about the party, and I wanted to go too. I needed some mercy and intervention to convince my mother to let me stay out late. She was the real disciplinarian of the house. If I cleaned the house spotlessly, she might be more lenient with me. My mother loved a clean place, especially hers.

I mopped, waxed, and buffered the hardwood floors, cleaned the bathroom with Clorox and pine-sol, and washed all the dishes. The house was immaculate, and I hoped that would impress my mom enough to change her mind about the curfew. But my mom was a drill sergeant and not easy to persuade. A no meant a no.

Once she and my dad made a rule about respecting the house rules, she expected everyone to stick to it. There was no room for negotiation or compromise. I learned that the hard way once when I came home late. She locked me out of the house for an hour before she let me in. Back then, when your parents said yes or no, they meant it.

I mustered courage and went to talk to my mom. She was in my bedroom ironing clothes and presumably talking to my dad. I hope she will appreciate my cleaning efforts and let me go to the party. Honestly, all my strenuous efforts were bribes to go to the party, and she could see straight through it.

While seeing my mother in my room was not strange, she often set up the ironing board there to iron the clean laundry. It was odd to see my father there in the room. He usually rested in the living room on the sofa. There were two twin beds located in my room. She was standing at the ironing board, ironing clothes and pressing them with starch. My dad was fast asleep and lying atop my twin bed. He never did that before. Was it a premonition or a sign? But I realized it was my grandmother's final resting place in my parent's house--my twin bed.

I still didn't put too much thought into him lying across my bed as I was too focused on pleading my case to leave the house at 11:00 p.m. to attend the dance.

"Mom, Gloria called and asked if I could attend a graduation dance. Everybody who's anybody will be there; the dance is for all graduates. The only thing is that the dance doesn't get hot and popping until around 11:00 p.m., so Gloria asked if she could pick me up at that time."

A quick response from Mom was, "No."

Unexpectedly, my father quickly interjected, "Annie Mae, let her go. Let her go to the dance."

My mother promptly rebutted, "That's what's wrong with her now. Every time we agree on something, you change it."

At this time, my father looked up from my bed and mildly but firmly said, "Annie Mae, let her go!"

I'd won the battle to attend the graduation dance. Thank you, Dad.

At the graduation dance, the music of Rolls Royce's "Car Wash," Earth, Wind & Fire, and Marvin Gaye's "Got to Give it Up," and others filled the air, and we were getting down on the dance floor and having the time of our lives at the graduation party.

I subconsciously knew it was getting late but hadn't realized it until Gloria returned to her parent's shiny, green Chevy Impala to spruce up her makeup. I noticed the time as she turned the key to "on" and the inside dome light to turn on. The car's clock showed 2:00 a.m., and panic struck me just like in the book Cinderella when her fairy Godmother instructed her to return home before a specific time, and she was running late.

Somehow, I knew I had to get home urgently. For what, I did not know. I emphatically told Gloria that I needed to return home immediately. Gloria replied that as soon as she put some lipstick on her lips and returned inside the building to give a boy her home telephone number, we would leave the dance. She lowered the car's mirror visor and continued putting on the lipstick. We re-entered the building, and then soon, she drove me home.

When Gloria and I arrived at my house, I quickly noticed my grandfather's blue Buick Electra 225 parked in front of the house. Still, with the adrenaline and excitement of getting to attend the graduation dance way past curfew and listening to Gloria's girlish chatting about how she met a potential boyfriend, I tried not to read too much into my grandfather's car parked in front of the house at this time of the night. It was still dark outside, but every light in my parent's house was on, including the porch and backside lights. It was the feeling that something out of the norm had just happened. My senses grew alert, "What has happened?"

Just as I noticed all the lights, a neighbor whose home was directly in front of my parent's house walked down her incline driving way, leaned over into the car, and admonished me that I needed to go inside the house. My immediate concern was my mama. O'God, what has happened to my mama? Had she taken ill? I exited the car and followed the neighbor up my parent's drive to the walkway leading to two steps to the porch. As I came to the door, I saw my mother's face. Mama? Thank God she's okay! My mother collapsed in my arms in a sobbing heap as we embraced each other. The announcement from her mouth had words I thought I would never hear.

"O' Darnella, your dad just died."

Stunned, frozen, and in disbelief, I stood there. I was suddenly grappling with the thought of losing a father—a complete void of comprehension.

How?

Why?

Daddy?

My DAD!

My grandfather was now at the door to embrace us soothingly, saying, "It's going to be okay."

The front door was now fully open; my eyes rested on my father lying motionless in my parents' bed. He was fully dressed and looked like he was just peacefully asleep. I heard the words again, "He just died."

I backed out of the house in disbelief. It could not register in my heart and soul that my father was gone.

"Ken, my father has just died," I announced over the telephone.

As I uttered these words, a ton of bricks seemed to fall over me. The loss of my father was too much, and the burden was too heavy.

Just saying, "My father died!" shifted me from feeling stunned and doubting the veracity of what I heard to actualizing what I was saying. The reality of my father's loss struck me hard, and I started running. My mother and grandfather grabbed me before my body crashed into a brick pillar on the side corner of the porch. I heard them consoling and comforting me, both repeating that it was "gonna" be okay.

I sobbed.

I cried.

I wept.

As my mother wiped the tears from my eyes, I asked, "When did he pass away?" Since my father's body was still in the house, I knew it had happened recently.

Without hesitation, my mother replied, "2:00."

I understand now why my father awakened from his sleep and infallibly allowed me to attend the graduation ceremony. God never puts too much on us than we can bear. There was no way for me to be at home and see the demise of my dear father. This was God's mercy. I know why I had to leave the dance at 2:00 a.m. It was the final gentle call of my father to come home and to see him for the last time, just as I knew him. I also understand now why my father lay on my bed just like my grandmother did. It was a way of saying goodbye to a loved one in this life. A message that said, "You are my treasure, and I love you more than words can say. Even though I must leave you now, please know that I always loved you and always will." "Goodbye, my darling."

"Even though I walk through the valley of the shadow of death, I will fear no evil, for you are with me; your rod and your staff, they comfort me." (Psalm 23:4)

"Blessed are those who mourn, for they shall be comforted." (Matthew 5:4)

"For I am sure that neither death nor life, nor angels nor rulers, nor things present nor things to come, nor powers, nor height nor depth, nor anything else in all creation, will be able to separate us from the love of God in Christ Jesus our Lord." (Romans 8:38–39)

Afflicted but not destroyed.—But God!

CHAPTER **10**

꧁꧂

Behold Thy Mother

*T*HIS IS PART of a verse from the Bible, in the Gospel of John, chapter 19, verses 25-27, when Jesus entrusted his mother, Mary, to his beloved disciple John and John to Mary. He said to his mother, "Woman, behold your son," and to the disciple, "Behold your mother." This shows his love, care for them, and fulfillment of the scriptures.

I, too, was entrusted to a mother as a child and a mother entrusted to me as my mother.

Maternal is an adjective meaning "having the quality of or befitting a mother." Though Annie Mae Fields was my father's wife, she was a mother to me.

She was barren, or what would now be known as infertile. Infertile is used in modern medical terminology for women who cannot bear their children. She raised me as her own from the moment my father brought me into their home. I tenderly called her 'Mama.' She was the only mother I knew from my toddler years to adolescence.

She affectionately cared for, taught, provided, and nurtured me through every runny nose, every bruise, every PTO school meeting, every school honor I received, and even spoke up for me against bullies. Being bullied was a common problem being raised as an only child. The neighborhood kids would think I had no one to back me up. Oh, they were so misinformed.

I remember being teased by bullies while heading home from school. These bullies were from the same family and out of the same household. It was alleged that this family burned one of their family members alive.

They had a mentally and physically challenged brother, which was no fault of his. His condition can be termed mild retardation coupled with a physical disability. The child was not permitted by his parents to attend school. Therefore, he would escape from home and roam around the neighborhood. I often saw him on the corner of Person Avenue and Gaither Street, the two emerging intersections where the school children would turn to the right to attend Pine Hill Elementary, the assigned neighborhood school. He would roam at least one mile to two miles from the house. He wanted to participate in school and leave the house for a while. Unfortunately, he never arrived at school, as he was always spotted, identified, and brought back home. His parents would then beat him.

One afternoon, while outside playing with the neighborhood kids, smoke began to billow from the neighbor's roof across the street house. Suddenly, sirens were blowing, and a herd of fire trucks was nearing the scene. As the firefighters arrived and entered the house, they brought out an opened red gasoline can. One fireman dragged two large and bulky chains down the neighbor's driveway. Two others carried a burned mattress with physical and notable fire damage to the center of it.

An ambulance arrived at the scene, and the emergency medical technicians brought out what appeared to be a body covered under a black plastic bag. All the kids who lived in the house could be accounted for and were standing in front of the house. Only the child who would wander off was missing.

I stood there in devastation, witnessing the entire episode and the potential of what just happened. The opened fire hydrants blasted cold water as the firefighters unsealed the fire hoses. Again, I stood on the sidewalk across from this house in utter shock at what I had just witnessed and tried to process everything.

Next came the news reporters and their camera crews from the local television stations. The parents were interviewed, and they stated their child had a history of running away, and today, the other children were playing and chained him to the bed.

They claimed the mentally and physically challenged child poured gasoline on himself and lit a match. They also told the news reporters that they had quickly run to the child's room and tried to extinguish the fire, but the bed was engulfed with flames making it impossible to put out the fire. The child was burned alive!

Hearing and witnessing this event was troubling. For the first time, I had a nightmare and experienced a sense of fear. I had never known fear and was not acquainted with having nightmares.

That night, I was afraid to open the fence gate to put my bicycle in my godmother's backyard. I felt fear for the first time and feared the darkness brought on by the night. My godmother lived adjacent down the street and two houses from my home. It was summer, and I lived at her home that summer while my mother worked out of town. I stood outside the closed gate, glancing into the backyard, piercing through the night's darkness, and feeling spooked to open the gate. I thought about the charred-skinned child; although he wouldn't be there, the thought was horror-stricken. I quickly pulled up the gate latch, barely opening the gate, only wide enough to give the bicycle a hard thrust to roll inside the entrance. I saw the green and white roll and wobble and then land on its side, far enough behind the house not to be seen by takers. I frantically pushed the latch back down on the gate and ran into my godmother's house.

When I went to bed that night, I had a nightmare that I was riding my bike in a neighbor's yard across the street and adjacent to the charred boy's house. In the nightmare, this neighbor's front yard was full of holes like deep tunnel well. They were in the shape of tunnel tubes created by oil drillers while drilling deep in the ground for crude oil. The wells were hollow and dark. As I rode my bicycle a second time around a pit well tunnel hole, this pit hole lit up, revealing a bottomless glass portal. The charred boy shot out from the bottom of a portal pit, grabbed my right leg, and tried pulling me down into the hole—an outburst of gruesome laughter exuberated from the boy as he pulled my leg. I screamed in desperation, shock, and terror. I did not desire to go down into the hellish pit. Help came from somewhere; I don't know who. The Help was unseen. With a sinister laugh but defeat, the dead boy released my leg and slid back down into the bottomless pit. The portal pit turned dark, and the glass turned into metal casking. I awaken with my eyes wide open and sweating from my head to my toes--visibly shaken.

From that night forward until I was an adult, I always slept with the cover over my head, waking up with part of my hair straight and the other part a fluffy afro from the sweating under the covers. I always slept with my head under the bed covers, even in the spring and summer.

Every day after school, I faced this same group of children from the house across the street. They were a mean bunch of bullies who taunted me until I was in tears. I abhorred walking home from school and tried not to linger at school after dismissals. But they would catch up with me, and the taunting would begin.

They were a large family. They were also a dangerous family with a dark reputation.

I eventually told my mother, Annie Mae Fields, what they did to me. She worked as a maid for a white family on Walnut Grove, where many big homes were located, and came home tired. But she was willing to take time and listen to her daughter.

After I had finished telling her about the torment from the bullies, she had enough. She told me to stay put and marched over to their house. She knocked on the door and faced their mother, who was as mean as her children. She said to her in an assertive and clear voice, "You better keep your football team on your side of the street, and you better leave MY daughter alone."

She said it with such authority and confidence that I felt a surge of pride and admiration for her. She didn't care who they were or what they could do to her. She was ready to fight for me, no matter what. She made it clear that I was HER daughter and you better leave her daughter alone.

My mother made many sacrifices for me. In the 60s and 70s, when Jim Crow laws were still in effect, black women had few opportunities. She had to work hard and long hours for little pay, but she never complained or gave up. She was grateful for her job and the family she worked for.

They were a wealthy family who lived in a big house with a pool and a trampoline in their backyard. They treated my mother well and liked her a lot. They even let her travel with them in the summer. They also liked me and welcomed me into their home. They never made me feel different or unwelcome because of my skin color. They saw me as a child (not black) but just as a child. Better said, they saw me as Annie Mae's daughter who deserved respect.

I had fun playing with their daughters, Susan, Kim, and Pam, who were around my age. We played games and swam in the pool together. We sometimes got rough and pulled each other's hair, but it was all good fun.

My mother reminded me once that I had to be careful pulling their hair, although we were playing, and they pulled mine. She knew that even though they were nice to me, they still lived in a different world than mine. A world where white people had more power and privilege than black people. A world where a black child could get in trouble for touching a white child's hair, especially if they cried. The situation could be blown out of proportion.

She always looked out for me and taught me how to survive in this world. She was a woman of wisdom and foresight. She helped me understand the cultural differences between whites and blacks and where to draw the boundaries in those times. But she never taught me racism or tolerated racism. It is not by skin color that we judge or make people our friends. It is by their character and how they treat us. But even if they treat us incorrectly, try not to fall into the rabbit hole of racism.

Nowadays, while I am not color-blinded, I still don't judge people by their skin color but by their character and actions. But I also remember where I came from and what my mother taught me.

My mother, Annie Mae Fields, was a selfless woman who always put others before herself. For some time, she had not had a coat that fitted her well; she wore my father's black wool coat. It was a lambskin wool coat; nevertheless, she needed her own coat.

She ensured my dad and I had a hearty breakfast every morning and a full-course dinner in the evening. As the Psalm says, she was a virtuous woman worth more than rubies.

Once, we were shopping at the Giant Food Store at the South-gate Shopping Center on Third Street in Memphis when a man who worked with her approached us. He looked at me and asked her, "Annie Mae, is this your daughter?" She smiled and nodded, her eyes shining with pride and love. She said, "Yes, this is my daughter."

She loved me so much, and I loved her too. That's why it broke my heart when I learned someone had betrayed her and changed her Will after she died.

My mother, Annie Mae Fields, died of colon cancer. Before her demise, the doctors tried to stop the progression of the disease with surgery and chemotherapy. However, signs and symptoms of recurrence began to appear shortly. The colon cancer recurrence aggressively spread to other parts of her body, mostly settling in her lungs and colon. The doctors said she had only a few months left to live. I received the call of her demise around 3:00 a.m. I rolled out of bed and fell to my knees.

She made a Will before getting sick, but someone changed it on her deathbed before she died. I was shocked, confused, and angry when I heard the new Will at the Probate Court. An aunt by the name of Emma said she was the executor of the estate. But I knew she was lying. She was the one who changed the Will.

God, please hold her in your arms
And let her feel your peace
Lord, she doesn't have to suffer anymore
But I still miss her so much
God, please comfort me in my grief
And help me find release

꧁꧂

CHAPTER 11

Looks Can Be Deceiving

"Trust not too much to appearances." – Virgil

$\mathcal{E}$MMA WAS A family member who lived in Jackson, Michigan. My beloved grandmother Mrs. Vienna Christian had two siblings, Aunt Emma and Uncle Curtis. Uncle Curtis lived as a sharecropper in Arkansas. Emma was my mother's aunt, Annie Mae Fields. She migrated north to Michigan in the early 1950s, during the Black Migration movement from the rural southern states to the northern. She was the youngest sibling and the spitting image of my grandmother, the same height and similar body frame. Both women wore glasses, and their voice tone was identical. The only outward noticeable difference between the two sisters was that Mrs. Vienna Christian, my grandmother, was adorned with blue silvery shimmer hair that she wore like a regal crown, gratefully.

My grandmother, Vienna Christian, was full of grace towards others, and God granted her the blessing to age gracefully. "For the Lord takes pleasure in His people; He will beautify the meek with salvation." Psalm 149:4

On the other hand, Emma was a wolf in sheep's clothing. She looked like my grandmother, but she acted like a serpent. Emma was cunning and deceptive, a green snake in the grass. She came to our home in Memphis pretending to be my mother's caretaker, but she was really a thief and a liar.

My mother was terminally ill and needed constant care. Emma claimed to care and offered to help. But she had ulterior motives. Emma wanted to get her hands on my mother's Will and insurance policies. She tried to rob me of my inheritance.

Emma did not care about my mother's well-being or comfort. She only cared about herself and her greed. She harassed my mother day and night, trying to get her to reveal her Will's location and change the beneficiary's name on her insurance policies.

My mother was too weak and sick to resist Emma's pressure. She was in pain and suffering, but Emma showed no mercy or compassion. She was like the false prophets who "speak lies in [God's] name" (Jeremiah 14:14). She tried to deceive my mother with half-truths.

Emma tried to convince my mother, Annie Mae Fields, that I was not her real daughter, that I had abandoned her for my biological family, and that I did not love or deserve her inheritance. She said some devious words to turn my mother against me, to make her doubt my loyalty and affection.

But my mother knew the truth. She knew I loved her with all my heart, was grateful for everything she had done for me, and would never leave or betray her. She knew that Emma was a false witness who "breathes out lies" (Proverbs 6:19). She knew that Emma was "a heart that devises wicked plans" (Proverbs 6:18).

My mother refused to listen to Emma's lies. She refused to tell her where her Will was or to change her insurance policies. She was steadfast in her integrity, even when Emma threatened and scorned her. She trusted God's promise: "Whoever walks in integrity walks securely" (Proverbs 10:9).

My grandfather was also aware of Emma's evil scheme. He tried to protect my mother from Emma's harassment. He told Emma the Will was in the car's trunk, but it wasn't true. He tricked Emma into searching one of the car's trunks, where she found nothing but a spare tire and stagnated water from the leaky trunk.

Emma was furious when she realized that my grandfather had misled her. She became even more relentless and vicious in her pursuit of the Will. She did not give up on trying to deceive my mother and me.

She tried to convince me that she had my best interest at heart and cared about me like my grandmother. She tried to lure me with sweet words, but deep in my gut; I knew something was wrong with Aunt Emma. I did not fully trust Emma. But I was swayed because she looked so much like my guardian angel grandmother.

Annie Mae Fields viewed Emma as her dear aunt who would be compassionate and sympathetic to her needs and affairs, especially during a life-threatening illness. However, Emma's true colors came shining through. The old familiar saying, 'What's done in the dark will come to light,' is true.

Emma eventually went to the point of hiring a shady lawyer to rewrite my mother's Will on her deathbed. My mother was incoherent. And even today, I pray that the original Will is released. Someone has it. I am not too concerned about the statute of limitation but knowing that my mother's true desires and wishes are vindicated.

It is a sin and shame how greed takes over the heart and minds of people at the time of the death of a loved one to acquire property and inheritance, and they are willing to take advantage of and hurt people by any means possible. "The Love of Money is the root of all evil" (1 Timothy 6:10), and the lack of money will cause people to take yours, and in some cases, they are those who claim to have your back and love you. In all things, stay prayerful.

Emma was a green snake in the grass and a deceiver, but God was my shield and defender. He protected me from her venom. Things could have been worst. Emma's vicious plan was that I would not receive a 'penny' from my mother's inheritance. But God, he was my refuge and my fortress, my God in whom I trust (Psalm 91:2).

CHAPTER **12**

๛

God Will Take Care of You
"Go Back to Memphis"

C ALL IT STUPID or naive, but after my mother's death, I could still not fully accept the truth about Aunt Emma's deceptive behavior. I staggered from time to time between two opinions of Emma's true character. I struggled. How could someone who resembled my grandmother, Mrs. Vienna Christian, who had the same gentle eyes and soft smile, be so cruel and manipulative? She had been my grandmother's confidante and close sister--her only sister. But she was a snake waiting for the right moment to strike.

I wanted to trust Aunt Emma. I wanted to believe she cared for us, to be a grandmother figure for me and a caregiver for my mother. But the 'proof was in the pudding'; she had a hidden agenda. She wanted to take over the family house and my inheritance and distort the last minutes of my mother's life. And then, one day, my mother was gone.

I was devastated by my mother's death. She had been my best friend, my role model, my everything. I blamed myself for being unable to save her from Aunt Emma's influence. I blamed myself for not seeing through all her fakeness. I blamed myself for not being a better daughter. I was in denial, in shock, in grief. I didn't want to believe that she was gone forever. And I didn't want to believe Aunt Emma was behind all the scheming and lies.

I couldn't ignore the truth for long, but I also found it challenging to accept it. I was desperately seeking the acceptance and love of a family. My beloved mother was gone.

Aunt Emma didn't waste any time taking over the house. She claimed my mother had left everything to her in the Will and that I had no rights or say about the place. She changed all the locks on the doors outside the home and sold most of the furniture. She defended her move, saying she changed the door locks to prevent others with keys from entering the house and taking items without permission. However, if truth be told, Emma was the thief. She acted like a deprived thief at best and a slivering snake. It was a nightmare. A nightmare that I refuse to wake up to at the onset and the ending of an evil plot.

The nightmare continued. Aunt Emma didn't care about money and fraudulently obtaining the house. After she sold all the furniture and changed the locks on the house, I retained a large antique armoire to hang my clothes and all of my mother's clothes for a loving keepsake of her memory.

Aunt Emma packed her bags and bought a plane ticket to return to Jackson, Michigan. She didn't invite me to go with her. She didn't care what happened to me. But I was desperate for a family, connection, and a home. I had lost my dad when I was seventeen and now my mom when I was nineteen. She was the only mom I ever knew. I felt alone and abandoned. So, I did something stupid and desperate. I bought a plane ticket, too, and followed Aunt Emma to Michigan.

I hoped that things would be different there. That maybe, Aunt Emma would be kinder and more generous there, that perhaps she would see me as her grieving niece, not an outsider. Maybe she would love me like my grandmother always did. Her sister, my grandmother, was my protector and guiding light. But I was wrong. As soon as we landed and I entered her home, I felt a coldness in the air. Aunt Emma looked at me with disdain and annoyance. She didn't want me there. She had lost her husband the year before and did not want anyone around her in the house. She was an old, selfish, and bitter soul.

But one person pitied my plight and showed compassion: Aunt Emma's daughter-in-law. She lived in a beautiful house in the suburbs. One day, she visited me at Emma's home; she invited me to stay with her for a while. She said she wanted to get to know me better and felt sorry for all I had experienced and what I had been through. She lovingly offered her condolences for the death of my mother.

She was kind and friendly, unlike her mother-in-law. I accepted her invitation and moved in with her and her family—her husband and three children. I thought maybe this was my chance to find a new family, to feel loved and accepted—a new beginning.

Emma's daughter-in-law, Lisa (I will call her), was empathic. She offered me her daughter's room. Lisa's house had four spacious bedrooms, and the daughter volunteered to stay in a bit more oversized bedroom. It was a win-win situation. The room Lisa offered me was beautiful, with elegant French provincial furniture that reminded me of my grandparents' main bedroom. I felt cozy and comfortable there.

Lisa introduced me to her mother, who lived in a big farmhouse by a lake in the rural suburb of Jackson, Michigan. I went fishing on the lake with Lisa's sons and quickly learned that fishing was not my forte. It was too dull to be drifting around in a boat, waiting for a fish to bite a hook. Again, not my thing. However, the house was peaceful and was nested in a scenic place, surrounded by nature. Her mother was also very kind and friendly. She invited me to stay with her anytime I wanted. She said she had plenty of room at her house. She hugged me and smiled at me. I felt loved and welcomed by her. Could this finally be the start of a new family for me?

After leaving Lisa's mother's home that day, Lisa and I had a heart-to-heart chat where she revealed to me the true intentions of Emma's heart. She related to me that Emma did not want me there. That is to say—in Michigan. I felt betrayed and hurt. My eyes began to open up. No more a nightmare, but reality. I stepped out of being in denial about Aunt Emma. I saw who she was and what her intentions were all along. I experienced all that, yet I continued to give her the benefit of the doubt. Her choices were not for my mother, nor were her intentions for me—my mother's child.

I remember going to sleep that night. Somewhere between the falling asleep phase and the profound sleep phase, a subtle thought came to my spirit, which seemed like a soft voice speaking to my heart. It softly whispered the words, *"Go back to Memphis."*

Granted, I knew this was not my thoughts or voice telling me to go back to Memphis because I was desperately seeking a family, and there was no family in Memphis for me. So, I questioned the voice, "Go back to Memphis for what?" "There is nothing in Memphis for me." Then the voice quickly and tenderly spoke back, but this time in a gentle directive— "Go back to Memphis because I am going to take care of you."

After receiving this comforting and authoritative message, I immediately booked a flight back to Memphis. Despite not knowing where to live now since Emma had changed the locks on my family home, I found solace in the generosity of Mrs. Bernice, a dear friend of my grandmother who kindly opened the door of her home to me.

I slept on Mrs. Bernice's living room sofa on my first night in Memphis. The couch was covered in clear plastic. Back then, some people used custom-made plastic covers on their sofas to protect the tapestry. They bought furniture to last for a lifetime, especially living room furniture. I was in a no-zone area, and a sitting area used only for special occasions—like holidays. These were the days before the invention of stain-resistant fabric, and true enough, a spill could ruin the material so that the sofas would be covered in protective plastic. However, the protective plastic could be problematic for sleeping.

Mrs. Bernice and her husband owned a red brick bungalow house with two bedrooms. However, their second bedroom was used to store security equipment and a police radio scanner. I couldn't imagine sleeping with a radio scanner broadcasting police audio 24/7.

It was challenging to cope with the loss of my entire family in just three years - my grandmother, father, and mother - I was grateful for the kind hospitality of Mrs. Bernice. Her open door and the invitation to sleep on the plastic-covered living room sofa was a much-needed gesture of love, respect, and acceptance that I yearned for as a nineteen-year-old trying to navigate life without a family unit. I slept on the plastic sofa—gladly. Mrs. Bernice's house was an open door.

Immediately after returning to Memphis, I got my old job back at Methodist Hospital on Central Avenue. I reached out to my former supervisor in the Radiology Department, and she immediately said, "Oh, yes, you can have your job back."

I recall waking up early in the morning to start my workday. And the result of sleeping on the plastic sofa was that one side of my hair would be a kinky afro, and the other would be straight like a Hawaiian soft perm. I looked like a hot mess, but I was thankful for the invitation and the warmness of Mrs. Bernice's spirit and her husband's generosity. Every day, I went to work with an afro hairstyle and straight—half and half.

I am grateful to God for caring for me on my return to Memphis. God keeps his word, and his words cannot fail. I was given a place to sleep immediately and without hesitation. Although God's route for me was to travel from pillow to post, each round got higher and higher. Despite facing many challenges, God led me each time to a better place on the journey. I think about Abraham and how he learned with each trial and challenge to trust and take God at His Word. He only considered what God had said and promised him. Abraham became fully persuaded through it all. "Go back to Memphis. I will take care of you," I remember the promise of God's words-the faith of Abraham.

When I first returned to Memphis, I slept on a plastic sofa, but a friend offered me a bigger and better accommodation - a bed. It may have been a twin-size bed, and I was genuinely grateful. The Bible teaches us about Abraham's unwavering faith in God's promises, which grew stronger with time. Abraham trusted that God was able to fulfill all his promises.

It may seem trivial to some, but sleeping on a bed instead of a plastic sofa was a powerful sign to me of God's faithfulness, His promise, and His unchanging words to provide for us. When we thank Him for the little things, God sees He can bless us with more amazing things, and our hearts will stay loyal to Him. God was taking me from one level of faith to another.

"Give thanks in all circumstances; for this is God's will for you in Christ Jesus." (1 Thessalonians 5:18)

"For in it the righteousness of God is revealed from faith to faith; as it is written, 'But the righteous man shall live by faith.'" (Romans 1:17)

I was grateful for my friend's mother's hospitality when she offered me a place to stay in their home. I slept in a twin bed in the same room as my friend and her sister, who were in a full-size bed. Despite sharing the space, I appreciated a twin-sized bed's open door and accommodation.

Another test of accommodations came within a year. Another test of trusting God at his words—"I am going to take care of you."

His wife shot my friend's oldest brother, and their four sons came to live with us. They had no other relatives who could take care of them. My friend's family was already big. She had thirteen siblings, some of whom still lived at home. The boys had to share the room where I slept, the only space available. My friend and her sister left the bedroom to sleep on the sofa in the front area of the house. They squeezed into the full-sized bed while I slept in the twin-size bed directly next to their bed. It was now crowded and noisy in the room. I didn't mind having the children in the room, but I felt uncomfortable sleeping in the same room with boys, of which two were teenagers. I was not used to these types of arrangements. And they snored so loudly that I could hardly sleep that night.

It was morning; the alarm clock went off, and I felt numb. It was time to get up and go to work. But I felt like I had barely slept at all. The boy's snoring had kept me awake for most of the night. I was so exhausted that I didn't want to move. I wanted to stay in bed and forget about everything. My spirit said, "Pray."

I mustered the strength to rise from bed and kneel beside my twin-sized bed to pray. I was overwhelmed with emotions, unable to articulate my thoughts, and tears were streaming down my face. I looked up towards the heavens and whispered, "LORD, you know, and you see."

After my prayer, I lay back on the bed, called in to work, and told them I would not report to work for the day. I was sleep deprived and bewildered by the entire sleeping arrangements.

I know that God hears an honest and fervent prayer because within roughly one hour, I heard the telephone ringing, and it was one of the mothers from the church calling for me. She was a prominent mother of the church because she was also the pastor's mother-in-law. She said she had called my job and asked for me, and they told her I was not there. She immediately called the telephone number where I was and asked me, "Darnella, what's wrong?" "It is not like you to miss work." "What's wrong?" I was startled because I had only shared my innermost hurts and thoughts with the LORD in a simple, honest prayer, so I was surprised she sensed I was going through a hardship even before I related all the details to her.

I shared with her the dilemma of my friend's family and the sleeping arrangement situation I was now a part of. She began interceding to the LORD by praying and calling out to LORD. "Oh, my God, have mercy!" The church's mother told me she would talk to her husband when he got off from work and call me back.

Early that evening, she gave a callback and told me she had spoken to her husband. They had an empty bedroom with a queen-sized bed, and she told me that her husband, a deacon and father of the pastor's wife, agreed that I could come and live with them. God now saw fit that I would have my own bedroom. From a plastic sofa to a twin-sized share with others, now to my bedroom with a queen-sized bed. God opened the door. And his promise—I will take care of you—became even more prominent. Again, it may seem small to some, but every round on the journey got higher and higher, and each step on the ladder only went from faith to faith. God is faithful.

As fate would have it, I was there for about a year and a half. Now, this family had a family emergency. The church mother's family had a dilemma in the family. Her son's wife was reenlisting in the army—which is good. The reenlisted soldier's husband was unemployed and struggling, which was the main reason for her rejoining the army. The couple had two small children. One child was an infant, and the other was a two-year-old toddler. Both children were sick with colds and flu. The parents could not afford the children's medical care. Therefore, the wife was reenlisting, and the husband was to follow the wife, leaving the children behind in the care of his mother--the church mother.

The church mother and her husband agreed to keep the children. This was family, and I understood. However, the only bedroom and now the only bed available was mine. Again, I welcomed the opportunity, but it was overwhelming. I did not mention anything because I was grateful for the open door. The church mother could see and read the dilemma on my face, although I never said anything. She saw accurately. She said she would give me time to find something to make me happy and soothe the overwhelmedness I was experiencing again.

I contacted a reliable source, the landlord of a former organist I dated at the church. He hailed from Ypsilanti, Michigan, and had relocated back to his hometown to reunite with his family. Knowing that the house he lived in Memphis was presently unoccupied, I approached Mrs. Matthews, his godmother, who was also his landlord. However, she regretted informing me that the house was currently occupied by Lonnie, a separated man in the process of getting a divorce and was seeking temporary housing accommodation. I was floored. I had no other options for housing and a place to live.

During this moment of despair, I recalled a conversation with Mrs. Matthews. She shared a heartwarming anecdote about Lonnie's love for his wife when I visited her home with the organist, whom she considered her godson. It seemed she wanted to share a joyous love story. She shared with me how deeply Lonnie cared for his wife and was always willing to go above and beyond to ensure his wife's happiness.

Upon receiving the disappointing news regarding the house's availability, great concern was raised in my spirit. I felt a pang of fear and anxiety. My only hope and dream was to stay in that house. It was the only house that I knew was available. Someone else had snatched it before me. I had been looking forward to getting out of the other home with the shared queen-sized bed and having a place I could call—home. I was ready to start a new chapter in life and go up another round in my faith walk with the

LORD. But now, my dream seemed to have all vanished. I didn't know what to do or where to go. I prayed to God for guidance and help. "Oh, LORD, where am I going?" "Oh, LORD, what am I going to do now?"

After receiving the devasting news and praying, I attended church the following Sunday and listened to a guest pastor's sermon titled "Stay on Board," based on Paul's shipwrecked voyage on the Maltese coast en route to Rome. Despite the shipwreck, Paul and most of the men on board reached the shore safely. During the sermon, the guest pastor began to speak the following words to the congregation:

"Whatever you want from God, see yourself receiving it."

I saw myself inside this specific house. I saw myself happily walking around inside this particular house on its pristine hardwood floors.

When I returned home that day from church, that night I prayed before retiring to bed. In my prayer to God, I wanted to make sure that my vision of this specific house was from the purity of my heart and that my motives were pure. I told God as I knelt and prayed to Him that I never wanted to have a selfish heart or pray a selfish prayer. I reminded God of Mrs. Matthew's conversation with me regarding Lonnie and how he deeply loved his wife. I prayed and asked God to fix it for Lonnie and reunite him with his wife.

"God, Lonnie loves his wife. Put them back together." "Fix it for Lonnie." "Fit it for them." "In the meantime, God, you see my need. I do not want to be selfish or pray selfishly, but I need a house." "God bless me with a house."

The deadline to leave the church mother's house was by the end of October. I will always remember that October has an extra day because of the miracle that happened to me.

"God is able to do exceedingly abundantly above all that we ask or think, according to the power that works in us." (Ephesians 3:20)

"Trust in the Lord with all your heart and lean not on your own understanding; in all your ways acknowledge him, and he will make your paths straight." (Proverbs 3:5–6)

"Behold, I am the Lord, the God of all flesh. Is anything too hard for me?" (Jeremiah 32:27)

I worked part-time at my church as the assistant secretary. I received a phone call while at work near the end of October. The full-time secretary announced, "Darnella, you have a telephone call."

I walked over to her desk and answered the call. When I said, "Hello," I immediately recognized Mrs. Matthew's voice. She stuttered and gasped, unable to form a coherent sentence. She was speechless and stunned by something that had just happened. She finally managed to say that she didn't understand what had happened so suddenly, but Lonnie had returned to live with his wife. They have reunited. She then went on to ask me if I still needed the house.

"Darnella," she softly said, "the house is available."

I was elated—elated! And stated to her a soft, "Yes."

We finalized the conversation: "The house is yours to move in."
"Darnella, the house is yours."

Mrs. Matthews informed me of the good news about moving into the house on October 29th. As a result, I could promptly move into the house on October 30th, meeting the crucial October 31st moving deadline.

I went from sleeping on a sofa with a plastic cover to a cozy twin-sized bed and then to a spacious queen-sized bed. Now, I had the luxury of choosing any spot in my home to rest--a completely furnished and finished house.

"Come to me, all you who are weary and burdened, and I will give you rest." (Matthew 11:28)

"The Lord is my shepherd; I shall not want. He makes me lie down in green pastures. He leads me beside still waters. He restores my soul." (Psalm 23:1–3)

"In peace, I will lie down and sleep, for you alone, Lord, make me dwell in safety." (Psalm 4:8)

Go back to Memphis because I will take care of you.

From pain to purpose.—But God!

༄༅༅

CHAPTER 13

Looking for the Answer

Nothing in life is to be feared, only to be understood. Now is the time to understand more, so that we may fear less.--Marie Curie

I DO NOT CLAIM to have any special knowledge or insight into the dark realm of witches and witchcraft. The very mention of the word makes me shudder, as I'm sure it does for most people; this memoir is not meant to be a tribute to the evil one and his wicked works. I only wish to recount some of the defining moments in my life that baffled and troubled me. Moments that I sought answers to understand so that I may fear less. Moments in my life that made me wonder why I was the target of such malice and hatred. In the span of two short years, I had suffered the loss of two precious souls: my grandmother, who was a guardian angel to me, and my father, who was my strong tower and protector. As Shakespeare wrote, "When sorrows come, they come not in single spies, but in battalions" (Hamlet, Act IV, Scene V). And as if that were not enough, someone was trying to hurt me even more. Why? What had I done to deserve such cruelty? As Job cried out in anguish, "Why is light given to him who suffers, and life to the bitter of the soul?" (Job 3:20).

You may be curious about what became of Yvette, introduced in the horrific event that began this memoir. I don't know. I only saw her once more when I returned to the Rust College campus, haunted by the memory of that dreadful night in my dorm room.

After leaving Rust at the end of the Fall semester and transferring to Memphis State University, I felt a strange urge to revisit the scene of the horror. I hoped seeing the place with my own eyes would help me understand what happened and could bring me some peace and stability back in my life.

Before that horrific event that night, I had always been confident and calm. Nothing could shake me or break me. I had never experienced such emotional turmoil or confusion. I will not say I had never experienced fear, but I was never acquainted with a spirit of fear. There is a difference. A spirit of fear desires to torment. It was a mystery that no doctor or counselor could solve for me. As Edgar Allan Poe wrote in a similar despair, "I was in sorrow unto death with a long agony" (The Pit and the Pendulum).

I drove down US 78 (Lamar Avenue) to Rust College on a sweltering summer afternoon. The campus was mostly deserted, as most students had gone home or taken summer classes elsewhere. I parked my car, got out, and walked toward the freshman dormitory, where it all began.

I greeted the den's mother, sitting at the desk in the foyer. She recognized me and permitted me to look around. I thanked her and headed down the familiar hallway.

As I walked, I recalled the faces of the girls I had met on my first day. We exchanged names and stories, laughing and bonding over our excitement of being first-year college students. Near the end of the hall, I turned left and saw the wall phone where I had hung up on Ken's call one night. I smiled at the memory of our young love and its growing pains. I kept walking.

Two steps forward, I saw a brown wooden door—the door to my first dorm room. I thought of my first-semester roommate, who had entered college with me. We were high school best friends, and both were accepted into Rust on an academic scholarship. We had been friends until she betrayed me over some fried chicken--when she flushed my portion down the dorm's toilet. No, thank you. I moved from our shared room to another room down the hall before we eventually came to angry blows because her anger continued to fester. And I knew I was one not to back down from foolishness. She had always been a dear friend of mine, and I did not want a potential drawn-out rift between us--especially not over fried chicken.

As I continued walking in the dorm that sweltering summer day, halfway down the right side of the hall, I saw another brown wooden door. I thought of Karen. She had been a true friend in my time of need. I smiled gratefully and thought of Proverbs 17:17: "A friend loves at all times, and a brother is born for adversity."

I passed the second bathroom and shower area on my left and took ten more steps from Karen's room. Then I saw it—the other brown wooden door that changed everything. My breath was caught in my throat, and my heart pounded in my chest. My thoughts became jumbled and anxious. The door was slightly open. With some hesitation, I pushed it open and stepped inside.

I scanned the room with a sense of dread. The walls, beds, bookshelves, and desks all looked familiar, yet a bit blurry. Then my eyes landed on the window—the source of my terror.

What had happened in this room that night? What monstrous thing had come through that window? Who was behind this evil plot? Why did they choose me? Why? Why? Why?

I backed out of the room, feeling more lost and confused than ever. I left the building with no answers, only questions.

I decided to take a short walk around the campus before leaving for good. I followed the paths I took every day and stopped in front of the Leontyne Price Library. I sighed with relief as I remembered how much I loved that place.

I pictured myself as a seventeen-year-old freshman, finding that secluded desk deep in the library, away from the noise and crowds, where I would study and read for hours. That was my happy place.

As C.S Lewis wrote, "We read to know we are not alone." Reading was my source of joy and wisdom.

I wished I could go back to those simpler times before everything changed.

I felt a surge of courage and self-assurance as I turned and walked briskly toward my car. Then I saw her—Yvette. She was standing there in the corner of my eye. Our eyes met, and I didn't know how to react. Should I speak to her? Could she be compassionate and provide me with clarification and answers?

Ignoring my inner turmoil, I approached her and exchanged greetings. I told her I had moved back to Memphis and would finish college there. She nodded and smiled with that same sly and wicked smile she had given me on that terrible night when Karen, her roommate, and the Oklahoma gang stormed into Yvette's room and demanded what she had put in the joint she had given me. She came downstairs with them and looked at me with a malicious grin. The same grin that now mocked me as we stood face to face. I shuddered.

That was the last time I ever saw Yvette.

I pray that Yvette has given up the Ouija board and her evil deeds. The Bible warns, "Do not turn to mediums or seek out spiritists, for they will defile you. I am the Lord your God." -Leviticus 19:31.

And as Shakespeare wrote,

"By the pricking of my thumbs, Something wicked this way comes." –Macbeth, Act IV, Scene I.

Little did I know then that Yvette had no passion for being compassionate. Also, little did I know she was a witch.

Afflicted but not destroyed: How God used my pain for purpose–But God!

CHAPTER 14

Five Ways to See God's Hand in Everything

HEN GOD'S HAND is on our lives, God is actively involved. God's hand represents his power, presence, and provision. We can see His hand in many ways, such as:

God's hand guides us. He leads us to his will and purpose for our lives. He gives us wisdom and direction. He helps us to make the right decisions and choices. Psalm 32:8 says, "I will instruct you and teach you how you should go; I will counsel you with my loving eye on you."

God's hand delivers us from our enemies and troubles. He keeps us safe and secure. Psalm 91:4 says, "He will cover you with his feathers, and under his wings, you will find refuge; his faithfulness will be your shield and rampart."

God's hand blesses us. He gives us good things and favors us. He satisfies our desires and needs. He grants us success and prosperity. Psalm 145:16 says, "You open your hand and satisfy the desires of every living thing."

God's hand heals us. He restores our health and wholeness. He comforts our sorrows and pains. Psalm 147:3 says, "He heals the brokenhearted and binds up their wounds."

God's hand empowers us. He strengthens us. He fills us with His Spirit. He equips us for service and ministry. Isaiah 41:10 says, "So do not fear, for I am with you; do not be dismayed, for I am your God. I will strengthen, help, and uphold you with my righteous right hand."

God's hand is on every person who loves him and follows him. He wants to show his love and faithfulness to us in every situation. As C.S Lewis wrote, "We may ignore, but we can nowhere evade the presence of God." We can see God's hand in everything if we have eyes of faith and gratitude.

God's hand overcomes the devil. He defeats our adversary and his schemes. He rescues us from his traps and temptations. He sets us free from his bondage and oppression. The devil cannot stop God's plan and purpose for our lives. He tries, but he cannot thwart God's hand on us. Romans 8:31 says, "What shall we say in response to these things? If God is for us, who can be against us?"

But God!

❧❧❧

CHAPTER 15

God is the Answer

OD SENT US the answer over two thousand years ago when he sent his only begotten Son, Jesus, to die for us on a rugged cross at Calvary. There is an old spiritual song titled "The Blood of Jesus Still Works." It is mainly sung on Communion Sunday. It goes something like this:

The Blood that Jesus shed for me Way back on Calvary
The Blood that gives me strength
From day to day
It will never lose its power.

It reaches to the highest mountain.
And it flows to the lowest valley
The Blood that gives me strength

From day to day
It shall never lose its power.

It soothes my doubts and calms my fears
And it dries all my tears
The Blood that gives me strength
From day to day
It shall never lose its power.

I do not own the rights to this song. I only have the right to my testimony that the Blood of Jesus stills works. The Bible declares in Revelation 12:11, "And they overcame him by the blood of the Lamb, and by the word of their testimony." I feel a shout right here--Glory!

God places the right people at just the right time on our path. He puts us where we need to be at the right time–the appointed time for the answer.

At the tender age of nineteen, I was in the Morning Star Holiness Church's welcoming arms at 3161 Park Avenue in Memphis, Tennessee. It was a new and unfamiliar place, but I needed refuge after losing the last surviving family member who raised me--my mother to a cruel fate. I had previously lost my beloved grandmother at the age of fifteen and my dear father at the age of seventeen. Though He slays me, yet will I trust Him (Job 13:15). I was trying to trust, yet it was much pain. And a pain that I could not understand the severity and frequency of its occurrence.

A young male Holy Ghost-filled minister joined the church. The church had never seen anything like this young minister.

He was on a higher spiritual realm than the entire congregation, including other ministers. He came in, speaking in tongues as the Spirit gave utterance and prophesying. This young man of God was on "Fire" for the LORD and the works of His God's Kingdom. As God would have it, this young minister had a strong attraction for me and wanted to marry me. I was reluctant; I was young and, most importantly, desperately and quietly seeking healing and deliverance from God–the answer.

Thank God this young man did not give up on his pursuit. But his desire for me was put there by God as part of the plan for the answer. He wanted me to meet his Spiritual mentor, who resided in Pontiac, Michigan. His mentor was known as the "Eagle Eye Prophet," likened to the Spiritual gifts and titles given to Prophet Isaiah in the Bible.

Soon, the Morning Star Holiness Church in Memphis buzzed with excitement and anticipation. A spiritual mentor, who had trained and inspired many powerful ministers, was coming to lead a revival for us. The pastor and the flock were overjoyed. We expected nothing less than a glorious encounter with the LORD through this anointed man of God. We invited the whole community to join us and witness the wonders and miracles of the Holy Spirit. And God did not let us down. God's presence filled the church and overflowed into our lives. People were healed, delivered, and set free from their bondage. New souls were added to the Kingdom of God. We had a fantastic time in the LORD that week. It felt like we were living in the Book of Acts, witnessing the apostolic power of God.

We went to see the Prophet at his hotel after the revival. The young minister wanted his mentor's blessing and approval for marriage. I was not seeking marriage but the answer for some pain and suffering. The pastor of Morning Star Church's eldest son came with us. The Prophet welcomed us warmly and kindly. We sat in awe of him, listening to his casual conversation and wise words. Suddenly, he shifted into a prophetic mode and looked at me with a piercing gaze. He said, "Sometimes we worry about things that will never happen."

He spoke right to my heart. I had been tormented by the memory of that terrible night at Rust. I felt guilty and ashamed for no reason. I felt like I was about to lose my mind. I silently suffered, hiding my deep emotional pain from everyone but the LORD.

We resumed our light-hearted talk and inquiries, led mainly by the pastor's son. He was eager to know about his marriage prospects, but the Prophet had yet to hear a word or answer.

The Prophet changed the topic and said he had to see a certain Prophetess before leaving Memphis and returning home. He said that she lived in a set of projects downtown. Most people used the term projects, without harm or ill-intent, for the government apartments where low-income people stayed. We gladly entered the young minister's car and drove to the Prophetess's home.

When we arrived, I saw a tall, thin woman in her middle years standing at the door. She greeted us all with a smile and hugged the Prophet warmly. She invited us into her home. We stood in the living room. The Prophet introduced her to us by name. The pastor's son started to bug her about his marriage plans. The Prophet cut him off and said, "Son, let's leave that on the back burner for now."

Then, in seconds, the Skekhinah Glory fell and filled the living room. Almighty God visited the projects that night. The Spirit was so strong and heavy that I could hardly stand. The Prophetess of God started to prophesy and announce, "God has ordained this night for you; that you may receive a deliverance."

I immediately fell prostrate on my back on the floor. Miraculously, I was not hurt or bruised as I fell under the presence of God's Holy Spirit on a concrete floor. God is so real. I was under the power and anointing of God's Holy Spirit. The Prophetess and the Prophet spoke with the authority of Jesus.

"Come out of her."

"Take your filthy hands off of her, satan."

"The Blood of Jesus is against you, satan."

I repeatedly kept hearing them say,

"The Blood of Jesus."

"The Blood of Jesus"

"The Blood of Jesus is against you, satan.

"The Blood of Jesus," in repetition.

I felt a newness, sudden lightness, and breath of freshness in my being. I opened my eyes while still lying on the floor under the anointing and presence of God's Holy Spirit. The entire surroundings seemed light with a new breath of fresh air.

As I lay there still prostrated in the presence of the LORD, I basked in the Holy Spirit, realizing that I had witnessed and experienced God's glory; and that He (and He alone) had worked a miraculous miracle in my life.

As I basked in God's glory, the Prophet asked me, "Who did this to you?"

My mind went blank as I did not want to fathom that anyone would summon devastating harm upon me. But I could see a particular person in my mind. That is when the Holy Spirit took over my tongues, and I began to speak in the Spirit.

The Prophet interpreted and said, "The Holy Spirit spoke through you."

"The Holy Spirit said, Yvette did this."

"She used witchcraft against you."

I was stunned and speechless. I felt it in my soul, but I couldn't believe that someone could be so evil to me. I knew I had enemies, but this was a whole new level of evil and lowliness. New levels, new devils. This one came from the deepest and darkest pit of hell.

Thank God for his grace and mercy. The Holy Spirit cannot lie, and God has the final say. His Word is Truth and Power. Jesus' Blood still works, and God is the–ANSWER!

Praise God. I thank God for saving, delivering, and making me the Woman of God I am.

CHAPTER 16

૭✿ᎧᏅ

Woman of God

"A woman of God may look like other women, but she is unique because she looks up to God in all that she does."– Gift Gugu Mona

$\mathcal{S}$HE WAKES UP early in the morning before the sun rises. She kneels by her bed and prays to God, thanking him for a new day and asking him to guide her steps. She opens her Bible and reads a passage, meditating on its meaning and applying it to her life. She prepares for the day, asking God what she should wear. She prepares breakfast for her daughter and greets her with a smile and a hug. She helps her child prepare for school and drives her there, praying for her safety and success. She goes to work, where she is a teacher and leadership leader.

She teaches her students with love and patience, sharing God's word and wisdom. She is respectful and kind to her colleagues and superiors, working hard and doing her best. She takes a break at noon and prays silently in her room. She prays for the school, the students, the staff, and the world. She goes back to work, finishes her tasks, and grades papers.

She leaves work and picks up her child from school, listening to her stories and encouraging her. She drives her to activities, such as gymnastics lessons and girl scout meetings. She cheers her on and supports her.

She goes home and cooks dinner for her family. She sets the table and calls everyone to supper. She thanks God for the food and asks Him to bless it and her family. She eats with her family, enjoying their company and conversation. She cleans the kitchen and helps with homework. She reads a bedtime story and tucks everyone in bed, praying and kissing them goodnight.

As she gets ready to sleep, she reflects on her day. While doing so, she silently endures the challenges she faces. Despite the struggles, she trusts God, trusting that everything will eventually turn out okay.

As she closes her eyes, she expresses gratitude to God for the day and prays for peaceful rest. She finds comfort in knowing God is watching over her and her loved ones, and she rests in His care.

God sees you, dear Woman of God.

❧❧❧

CHAPTER 17

All Things Work Together for the Good

Romans 8:28

The Bible declares, "And we know this."

OMANS 8:28 IS one of my favorite scriptures because it shows that no matter the difficulties, heartaches, and pain we experience, God has a way of turning everything around for our good. It's working for our good. God yet sits on the Throne. He rules, overrules, and causes everything to come out for the good of those who love Him. My life and I believe others reading this memoir bear witness to God's providential watch and care. If you do not know this, I invite you to accept a loving Heavenly Father into your heart. God will make things beautiful in His time. (Ecclesiastes 3:11)

My late pastor, Bishop W.A. Sesley, who has now transitioned home to be with the LORD, once preached a sermon entitled "Gambaru" (Never Ever Give Up). He preached that it is through our struggles that we reach our destiny.

Bishop Sesley brought out the illustration of a caterpillar that had now turned into a butterfly. He told how a man found a cocoon of a butterfly and watched it for hours as it tried to squeeze out of a small hole. The man pitied the butterfly and decided to help it by cutting the cocoon, but he did not realize that the struggle was necessary for the butterfly to develop its wings. The butterfly came out with a swollen body and shriveled wings; it never flew. The man learned that sometimes struggles are what we need to grow and become strong—struggling to escape the cocoon. When the butterfly got out, it tried to fly but could not because its strength was built and predicated on the struggle. When the butterfly struggles, it comes out of the cocoon whole and complete before schedule with no struggle; there is no victory. But it flies when the butterfly comes out in due time and season. When it comes out, it's beautiful.

Bishop Sesley used this metaphor in his sermon to teach us about life and personal growth. It teaches us that we should not avoid or escape from our challenges but face them with courage and faith. It also reminds us that sometimes we should not always interfere with other people's struggles but let them learn valuable lessons from their experiences. Most importantly, it shows us that

God has a purpose for our struggles and will help us overcome them if we trust Him.

The Bishop then compared the butterfly's struggle to Paul's thorn in the flesh and how the Biblical Apostle prayed to the Lord three times. Paul sought the Lord thrice and asked the Lord to remove the struggle. He said, "Three times I pleaded with the Lord about this, that it should leave me." (2 Corinthians 12:8)

Paul asked the Lord to take away whatever was afflicting him. God answered Paul, "My grace is sufficient for you, for my power is made perfect in weakness." (2 Corinthians 12:9)

When you need Him the most, God will speak to you and tell you that His grace is sufficient for you. He will say, "My grace is sufficient for you, for my power is made perfect in weakness." (2 Corinthians 12:9). In other words, Gamaru–means never give up.

"I will never leave you nor forsake you." (Hebrews 13:5)

"Fear not, for I am with you; be not dismayed, for I am your God; I will strengthen you, I will help you, I will uphold you with my righteous right hand." (Isaiah 41:10)

I pray that this memoir gives you hope and encouragement.

That God has an appointed time for your blessings, healing, and deliverance—a time preordained for you. As the Bible says, "He has made everything beautiful in its time." (Ecclesiastes 3:11). God knows the end from the beginning, and he has a plan and a purpose for your life. As Jeremiah 29:11 says, "For I know the plans I have for you," declares the Lord, "plans to prosper you and not to harm you, plans to give you hope and a future."

God is faithful, and he will not let you down. As Psalm 34:19 says, "Many are the afflictions of the righteous, but the Lord delivers him out of them all."

God is your healer and your deliverer, and he will do it in his perfect timing. As Isaiah 40:31 says, "But those who wait on the Lord shall renew their strength; they shall mount up with wings like eagles; they shall run and not be weary; they shall walk and not faint."

God bless you. "And may the LORD bless you and keep you; The LORD make His face shine and smile upon you, and be gracious to you; The LORD lift His countenance upon you, and give you peace."

Numbers 6:24-26 NKJV

Afflicted But Not Destroyed: *How God Used My Pain For My Purpose*

LIFE LESSONS

❧❧❧

The Power of Suffering

HE NEW PASTOR of Morning Star Holiness Church in Memphis, Terrance Boykin Sesley, the son of my beloved bishop who passed away, delivered a powerful message on "The Power of Suffering." He said that suffering has a purpose in our lives. He said suffering can strengthen our faith and bring us closer to God. He said that suffering is not something we should avoid or resent but embrace and endure with God's grace. His words were true to God's Will and plan and were a good fit for a teaching moment and the genuine concept of my memoir. I want to share the content and truth of his sermon that suffering is valuable and a part of our journey with the LORD.

Pastor Sesley shared a story about a mysterious artist who could carve impressive statues out of wood. He said he once saw the artist sculpting downtown in Memphis with a piece of wood and a chisel, but the pastor did not see a picture or model the artist was following to make his sculpture. He was curious about how he did it and watched him work. He was amazed by how the artist transformed the wood into a beautiful sculpture with every detail and expression. He couldn't help but ask him, "How do you do this without a reference?" The artist smiled and said, "I had the image in my mind."

Imagine you're a sculptor with a piece of wood and a chisel. You don't have a picture to follow, but you have a vision in your mind of what you want to create. That's how God works with us. He holds our lives in one hand and a chisel in the other, and He has a plan for us that only He knows. He uses the chisel of suffering to shape us into the image He wants us to be. It might hurt, but it's for our good. Our lives are like works of art in God's mind.

No one likes to suffer; we do not like trials and tribulations. Many of us do not want to go through hard times. But through those hard times, God pulled something out of us that we did not know was in us. He births faith within us.

We may think that suffering is a curse, a punishment, or punitive. But suffering can be a blessing, a teacher, or a catalyst for growth. Suffering can show us what really matters in life, what we are capable of, and what we need to change. Suffering can make us more compassionate, more resilient, and more grateful. Suffering can transform us into better versions of ourselves if we let it.

Suffering is a way of getting closer to God. When we face hard times and challenges, the book of James in the Bible tells us, "Count it all joy..." We don't have to wait for the perfect moment to be joyful. We don't have to be wealthy or successful to be optimistic. We don't have to have everything under control. James said that when we are in our struggles and difficulties, that's when we should praise and thank God the most.

We often get it backward; we show up to church when things are good, but we turn away from God when things get tough. But what if we did the opposite and praised Him for the hard times too? We need to realize that the same God who allows us to suffer is the same God who will deliver us from it. "Weeping may endure for a night, but joy cometh in the morning" (Psalm 30:5). Let's rejoice in our trials and tribulations.

James didn't mince words when he told us that suffering is inevitable. We can't escape it in this life. It's not a matter of 'if' but 'when.' And it's not just one or two hardships, but many. We barely recover from one sickness, and another one strikes. We hardly pay off one debt, and another one piles up. We barely make peace with one foe, and another one shows up. New levels... new devils. We barely sort out one child, and another one acts up. We face many trials. We face many temptations. We face many troubles. We face--many. But here's the good news: we can rejoice in all of it.

Suffering can strengthen us because it shows us how much we trust God. The Greek word for patience is **ypomoní**, which means to endure a heavy burden. It means we don't give up on God even when facing hard times. The pain we feel is part of the journey but also helps us grow. It teaches us to endure. Every follower of God needs endurance to overcome the challenges of life.

According to the pastor's sermon, endurance affords us three things. They are as follows:

First, endurance is connected to how God rescues us. Matthew 24:13 says that those who endure to the end will be saved. God promises to deliver us from our troubles if we don't give up. He will come to our aid if we keep holding on. Don't lose hope; wait a little longer on God. God will rescue you.

Second, endurance is related to how God regards us. Hebrews 12:7-8 says that God disciplines us as his children. Those He does not correct, he does not care about. God does not waste his time with illegitimate children. God says if you are His child, He can discipline you, and if you can endure, you are His child. If we can endure, God considers us as one of His own.

Third, endurance is linked to how God rewards us. James 1:12 says that those who endure temptation will receive the crown of life. God has prepared a special prize for those who remain faithful to Him. He will honor us with eternal life if we resist the devil. He will crown us with glory if we stay loyal to him. Don't give in; fight a little harder. God will reward you.

Again, endurance is how God rewards us. James 1:12 says: "Blessed is the one who perseveres under trial because, having stood the test, that person will receive the crown of life that the Lord has promised to those who love him." This verse tells us that endurance is not just a passive acceptance of suffering but an active resistance to evil and faithful obedience to God. It also assures us that endurance has a reward: the crown of life, which is not a literal crown but a symbol of eternal life and joy with God.

Endurance is difficult, but God's help and grace make it possible.

He gives us the strength to face our trials and the hope to overcome them.

He also gives us love to motivate us and comfort us.

Endurance is how God rewards us, but it is also how we show our love for him. We endure because we trust him, we obey him, and we want to please him. We persist because we know Christ suffered for us on the cross and will never leave or forsake us. We endure to the end. It is not over until God says it is over. But we are guaranteed to win in the end. The fight is fixed in our favor. We are more than conquerors in Christ Jesus.

Finally, suffering is a way of growing and improving ourselves. We must be patient and let the process make us better and more fulfilled. Being perfect does not mean being flawless. It means being mature and complete. It means we have learned from our experiences and don't let them affect us negatively. For example, if someone ignores me or steps on my shoes, I don't get upset or take it personally. I know they have their own issues, and why make their problems mine? I genuinely pray for them and move forward in life. My goal is maturity, not taking things personally. Why would someone be rude or mean to you if you didn't do anything to them? They must be miserable in some way. Don't let them drag you down to their level. Misery loves company. Please don't join them in their misery. Don't engage. Also, when love leaves the table, it's time to get up and find a better table.

We must become more focused and grounded on what really matters in life. Petty and frivolous things don't matter. Suffering makes you a better person.

The pastor also references an experience he had at a jewelry store. He asked the jeweler what the most expensive item he had in the store was. Not that he was going to buy the item, but he had an inquiry mind to ask the question. The man took him to a vault in the store's back. The jeweler took out an expensive and exquisitely made pearl necklace. The pastor then asked what made this necklace much more valuable than anything else in the store.

The jeweler explained that this necklace was made of natural South Sea pearls, which are rare and highly sought after. He said that these pearls are naturally golden or white in color, and they have a beautiful luster and nacre quality. He also noted that these pearls are much larger than others, costing up to $100,000. The pastor was amazed by the beauty and value of these pearls, and he wondered how they were formed.

The jewelry stated, "Young man, you got to understand something." "These pearls were developed out of pain."

The pastor asked, "What do you mean by that?"

The jeweler explained that when the oysters get annoyed and bothered by foreign things and bugs that get inside their shell. Then, all of a sudden, to deal with the annoyance and frustration, the oyster starts to protect itself by covering the parasites with layers of nacre, the same stuff that makes the shell shiny and colorful. These layers of nacre make a pearl. The most valuable gems we admire to this day.

Life can be tough sometimes, but we can learn a lot from oysters. They have a unique way of dealing with things that irritate them. When something gets inside their shell, like a piece of food or a parasite, they don't just ignore it or get angry. They cover it with layers of shiny nacre, which their shells are made of. This is how they make pearls, which are beautiful and valuable gems. God works similarly with us. He can use our pain, frustrations, and adversities to make us stronger and more precious. He has grandiose plans for us that we can't even imagine. As the Bible says, "No eye has seen, no ear has heard, and no mind has imagined what God has prepared for those who love him." (1 Corinthians 2:9)

I know it's hard to endure tough times, but I want you to remember something: God has a plan for you and is using your suffering and pain to shape you into the person He wants you to be. He is refining your faith like gold in the fire and will reward you with His praise, honor, and glory. Your suffering is not in vain; it is producing endurance, character, and hope. And you are not alone; God loves you and has given you His Holy Spirit to comfort you and fill your heart with peace that passes all understanding. You shall come forth more precious than gold and as valuable as an oyster's pearl. So don't you dare give up, but rejoice in your sufferings and trust that God is working it all for your good and His glory. As the Bible says, "We know that in all things God works for the good of those who love him, who have been called according to his purpose." (Romans 8:28)

Let God use your pain for His purpose. You shall receive glory after this.

❧❧❧

Power of Forgiveness

"Forgiveness is giving up all hope of a better past." – Anonymous

*W*E CANNOT CHANGE past occurrences, but sometimes we cling to emotional hurts with the unrealistic hope that we can undo the past and make things better. We may hold grudges against people who have wronged us, regret decisions that we have made, or wish that we could erase painful memories. However, these emotional grievances only keep us stuck in the past and prevent us from moving forward.

During an interfaith memorial service, Reverend Don Felt, pastor of the Iao Congregational Church in Maui, shared a powerful message about forgiveness: "Forgiveness means letting go of the hope for a better past." Although it is still determined if Felt originated this phrase, it has been attributed to various sources.

Forgiveness is important because it allows us to move on from past hurts and heal from emotional pain. There are many stories of forgiveness in the Bible. Here are some examples:

- The story of David committing murder and adultery and being confronted by Nathan the prophet (2 Samuel 11-12)

- The story of Jacob and Esau reconciling after years of conflict (Genesis 33)

- The parable of the prodigal son who returns to his father's love and mercy after wasting his inheritance (Luke 15:11-32)

- The story of Joseph who forgave his brothers who sold him into slavery and saved them from famine (Genesis 37-50)

These stories show us that forgiveness is essential to our lives as Christians. It helps us to heal from emotional pain and move on from past hurts. It also allows us to show love and mercy to others, just as God has shown love and compassion to us.

Joseph's story in the Bible was a powerful example of forgiveness that helped me overcome my emotional pains and hurts.

In summary, Joseph was sold into slavery by his brothers and taken to Egypt, where he became a servant in Potiphar's house. Later, he was falsely accused of rape by Potiphar's wife and thrown into prison. However, after interpreting Pharaoh's dreams, Joseph was appointed Egypt's governor.

After many years, Joseph's brothers traveled to Egypt to purchase grain during a famine. However, they were unaware that the man they were dealing with was actually Joseph. Joseph accused them of spying to test his brothers and required them to bring their younger brother Benjamin to him. Once Benjamin arrived, Joseph revealed his true identity and forgave his brothers for their past actions.

In Genesis 50:19-20, Joseph reassured his brothers not to fear him. He acknowledged their past intentions to harm him but believed God turned it into good, saving many lives. Joseph's compassion for his brothers was evident as he generously provided for them and their families during the famine.

After hearing Joseph's story, I realized forgiveness was crucial for restorative healing, survival, and peace. Despite the emotional pain, it's essential to forgive. Moreover, Joseph's story demonstrates that God can bring good out of the worst situations, but we must trust Him.

I have forgiven my siblings for all the pain and sorrow they have caused me, as written in this memoir. It's possible that they don't agree with everything that happened or the consequences of their actions, but this is my story and my truth. Whether they meant to hurt me, I have chosen to forgive them. This decision has led me to a deeper understanding and connection with God despite my painful experiences. There is no space for hate or grudges in my heart. The choice not to forgive only hurts the victim. I choose not to become a victim but rather and victor. The power of forgiveness is vital.

The book of Genesis states that Joseph named his first son Manasseh, a Hebrew word that means "forgetting" or "causing to forget." Joseph chose this name because he believed God had helped him forget his troubles. This act of forgiveness is a decisive first step in transformation. God can help us forget our troubles and ease the pain of past events. Although the memory may remain, the pain subsides. As Teddy Pendergrass once sang, "It don't hurt now." "There are no more sleepless nights, heartaches, or fights."

Joseph named his second son Ephraim, which means "fruitful" in Hebrew. This name symbolizes Joseph's unwavering trust in God's ability to bless him despite his struggles, as stated in Genesis 41:52.

God blessed Joseph in the land where he suffered and was sold as a slave, the place of his suffering and crushing. Nonetheless, Joseph chose to forgive everyone, including his brothers, Potiphar's wife, and the cup-bearer who initially forgot to mention him to Pharaoh. God has a specific timing for our healing and deliverance. He blessed Joseph abundantly to the point where his cup overflowed.

Like Joseph, forgiveness can lead to prosperity and significant personal growth. I have experienced this growth after choosing to forgive, and I lack nothing. God has caused me to never want for anything. It is the LORD's doing and the LORD's blessings. Forgiveness is beneficial and wise to choose; it only leads to a blessed and peaceful life. Amen

Joseph's quote from Genesis 50:20 highlights that God can turn even the worst situations into something positive if we have faith in Him. This demonstrates forgiveness's third and final aspect, transforming and renewing our minds. Romans 12:2 also speaks to this, urging us not to conform to the world but to renew our minds to understand God's Will and purpose. Joseph did not complain about his circumstances but instead chose a growth mindset to overcome his challenges with God's help. He endured pain and suffering, relying on God's providence and provisions.

I also persist through pain and suffering, relying on God's providence and provision. Although it was initially difficult, I forgave during the process. As I grew in my faith and saw God's hand move, I realized that although others may have meant harm, God meant it for my good. I am blessed even more because of my pain and suffering. God turned it to support my purpose to help many.

Forgiveness can be complicated, especially when deeply hurt or betrayed. It means releasing your anger and resentment towards the person who harmed you and showing them kindness and understanding. Forgiving someone can bring you benefits such as letting go of bitterness, healing your emotional pain, and repairing your relationships.

Forgiveness has no specific formula, but several steps can be beneficial. Experts and researchers suggest some additional steps to practice forgiveness, which are as follows:

- It's essential to acknowledge and validate the pain caused by the offense. Allow yourself to feel the emotions associated with the wrongdoing, and don't try to deny, minimize, or suppress your feelings. Find healthy ways to express them, like talking to a trusted friend, writing in a journal, or seeking professional help.

- Choose to forgive. Make a conscious choice to release your resentment and opt for forgiveness as a means of healing. This doesn't imply that you approve or pardon the wrongdoing or forget or reconcile with the perpetrator. Instead, it indicates that you're prepared to let go of the adverse emotions and ideas hindering your progress and move forward with your life.

- It's essential to process your emotions. Take the time to grieve, express your anger, and deal with the pain before considering forgiveness. Remember, forgiveness is a journey that may require time and effort, and it's okay to revisit your emotions and decision multiple times before finding peace and closure.

- Shifting your perspective and viewing it from a different angle can be helpful. Consider the context, circumstances, and motives of the person involved. This doesn't mean you condone their behavior, but it allows you to empathize with their feelings and thoughts at the time. It's essential to recognize their humanity and complexity.

- To be kind and fair, it's important to empathize with others. Try to imagine how you would feel if you were in their situation. Remember that everyone makes mistakes and deserves forgiveness. Even if they don't ask for it or seem to earn it, extend kindness and mercy to them. Treat others the way you would want to be treated.

- After processing your emotions and changing how you view the situation, it's time to release the person who wronged you from your anger and resentment. It's also important to let go of any guilt or shame you may feel for being hurt or holding a grudge. Leave the past behind and concentrate on the present and future. Additionally, it's helpful to release any expectations or demands you had for the person, such as an apology, explanation, or change in behavior.

- It's essential to make amends and apologize, even to yourself, after a conflict. If appropriate, try to repair the relationship with the person who caused the conflict by making amends or apologizing for your own actions. It's also important to apologize to yourself for any negative self-talk or self-blame you may have engaged in and forgive yourself for any mistakes or regrets. Accepting yourself as you are is crucial.

- Take the time to celebrate the act of forgiveness. Acknowledge the positive impact it can have on both yourself and others. Recognize your bravery, resilience, and personal growth as someone who can forgive. Please share your story of forgiveness with those who may benefit from it and express gratitude for the chance to learn and become a more compassionate and forgiving individual.

This chapter on the benefits and steps involved in forgiveness will help you practice forgiveness. You may also find it helpful to check out online resources that offer guidance on forgiveness. May you experience peace and healing through the power of forgiveness. God bless you.

֍֎֎

Powerful Affirmations:

I CAN Statements and Motivational Thoughts:

- It's time to release any beliefs and negative energy that don't serve my higher self. Let's make room for positivity and growth!

- It's time to bid farewell to things that no longer do us any good - be it old thoughts, people, or habits.

- Stop overthinking! It's like trying to justify something that doesn't need explaining.

- Sometimes, it's okay to relinquish control and just let things be.

- Sometimes, it's best to let go and stop trying to force things to happen.

- Sometimes, it's best to release our worries and trust that everything will work out as it should. Allow God or the Universe to take care of the rest.

- Relax and have faith in God to take control.

- I acknowledge that chattering thoughts can be challenging to stop, but I can recognize them and let them go.

- I cannot control everything that happens to me. I can only control how I respond to them.

- It's important to avoid judging your thoughts and staying neutral to maintain healthy relationships.

- It would be best if you were not too hard on yourself.

- It's okay to have vices; you're not alone! Don't be too hard on yourself.

- It's always good to remember that moderation is essential in all aspects of life.

- Go ahead and order a refreshing Margarita or two.

- It is okay to listen to calming and uplifting music.

- It's okay to watch a favorite movie.

- Do not let other people's negative thoughts about you affect your life.

- It is essential to place a significant emphasis on self-love as well as appreciating love within other relationships.

- It is crucial to recognize your worth and not be influenced by inaccurate opinions that others may have of you.

- Why should I be concerned about what others think of me? They don't truly know me or even themselves. If they did, they wouldn't be so preoccupied with my actions. Those who truly know me will appreciate my skills, talents, and abilities.

- It's not my concern to worry about what people think of me.

- I am who God says I am.

- I am truly a sight to behold! I am crafted by the divine and fashioned in His likeness.

- I radiate a beautiful light and stunning glow.

- I exude a radiance that comes from within, a gentle spirit that shines bright.

- My mission is to spread brightness and enlightenment to those around me and the world.

- I am always ready to share my knowledge and help anyone who crosses my path.

- It's great if they decide to become enlightened; if not, it's their issue, not mine. Let it go.

- It's not within my power to make someone see the Light.

- It's not within my capabilities to save anyone. Only Jesus has the power to do so.

- My purpose is to spread hope and knowledge and bring Light to those around me.

- All caretakers take care of yourself first.

- Honor yourself.

- Always remember to honor your innermost being. It is essential to take care of your soul and treat it with the utmost respect it deserves.

- Stay true to your purpose.

- As a spiritual being, it's essential to recognize and honor my true self.

- To thy own self, be true.

- The truer I am to myself, the more freedom I have in life.

- I am free to be true to myself without pressure to conform to anyone else's false expectations.

- I realized that negative and contrary patterns do not serve my higher self or me. It's best to let them go.

- I will release anything contradicting my Spirit, soul, values, and beliefs. Let it go.

- Finally, meditation can be a helpful way to let go and clear your mind. Although there are various types of meditation practices, they tend to follow similar steps. If you're interested in trying meditation, here are some basic steps to get started:

- Choose the meditation technique that best suits your goals and preferences. Several options include mindfulness, mantra, or loving-kindness. Be mindful of the body itself.

- To begin, find a comfortable position. This can be sitting in a chair, on a cushion, or on the floor. Ensure that your spine is straight and your shoulders are relaxed. If you prefer, you can lie down but try not to fall asleep.

- To begin meditating, set a timer for 5 to 10 minutes or a shorter period if you prefer. As you become more at ease with the practice, you can gradually increase the duration of your meditation sessions.

- Try closing or resting your eyes to minimize distractions and concentrate on your thoughts. If you prefer to keep them open, focus on a neutral spot before you.

- Take slow and deep breaths while observing your natural breathing pattern. Observe how your chest and abdomen move with each breath. If your mind wanders, gently redirect your focus back to your breathing. Take deep a deep breath and exhale. Be mindful of your breath and your heartbeat. To enhance your mindfulness practice, consider listening to gentle, soothing music and focusing on breathing.

- Let's start the session by cultivating gratitude. Take a moment to meditate on all the blessings we're grateful for. It's a beautiful way to shift our focus from what we lack to what we have, and it can bring a sense of peace and contentment to our hearts. So, let's close our eyes, take a deep breath, and allow ourselves to feel thankful for the blessings in our lives.

- What are some of the things that we value and hold dear? Take a moment to appreciate and reflect on the beauty of these things.

- Find your inner guidance by connecting with the seat of your soul: your heart.

- This is a space free of judgment where you feel fully accepted.

- Take a moment to appreciate the stunning Light that radiates from above and shines upon your soul.

- With the guidance of the Holy Spirit, I have gained a deeper understanding of my true identity as a soul.

- His presence is the Light of my soul.

- The Holy Spirit wants us to be aware of Him. Connecting with His Light is the essence of our existence. It's what makes us whole and complete. It is with Him that we move and have our being.

- Fill my heart with your beautiful Light, Holy Breath.

- Breath

- Hold 1,2,3,4

- Exhale

- Letting it go, letting it go...

- Now, envision a happy place.

- Let it ALL go.

After completing your meditation session, taking a moment to rest is essential. When the timer ends, avoid the urge to get up immediately but take some time to express gratitude to yourself for dedicating time to self-care.

The Bible contains scripture that advises us to trust the Lord wholeheartedly and not rely solely on one's understanding. It suggests submitting to Him in all aspects of our life, and in turn, He will guide one's path in the right direction. This scripture can be found in Proverbs 3:5-6.

This life lesson is intended to assist you in initiating the process of letting go and harnessing its power.

www.ingramcontent.com/pod-product-compliance
Lightning Source LLC
Chambersburg PA
CBHW070708130626
46553CB00005B/1890